D0708146

WALTHAM FOREST LIBRARIES

904 000 00415088

indigo

dye it, make it

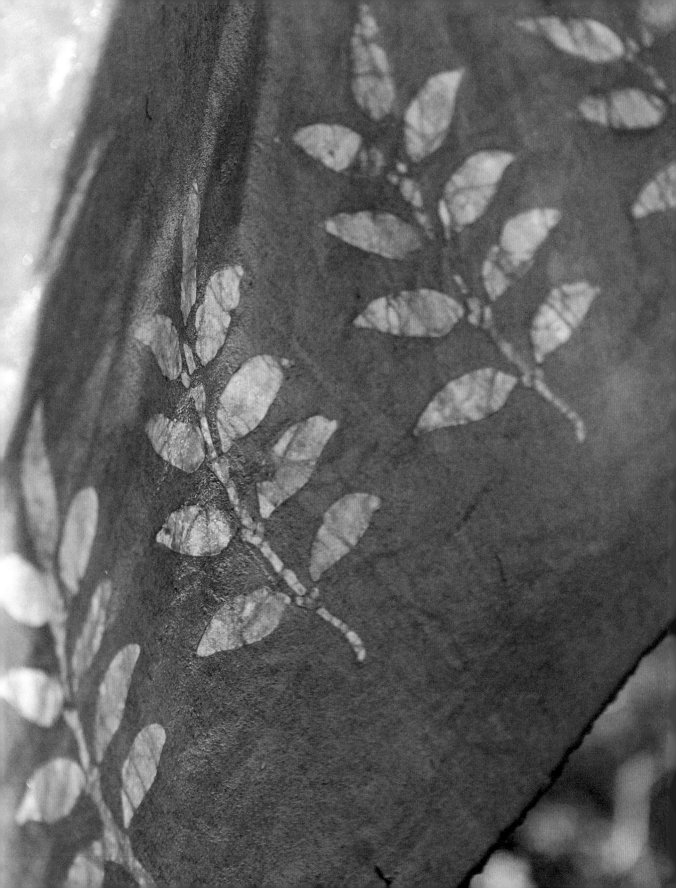

indigo
dye it, make it

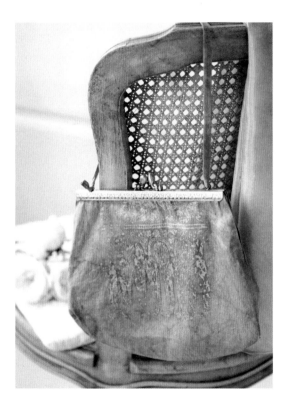

Nicola Gouldsmith

CICO BOOKS
LONDON NEW YORK
www.rylandpeters.com

Published in 2014 by CICO Books
An imprint of Ryland Peters & Small Ltd

20–21 Jockey's Fields   341 E 116th St
London WC1R 4BW   New York, NY 10029

www.rylandpeters.com

10 9 8 7 6 5 4 3 2 1

Text © Nicola Gouldsmith 2014
Design and photography © CICO Books 2014

The author's moral rights have been asserted. All rights
reserved. No part of this publication may be reproduced,
stored in a retrieval system, or transmitted in any form or
by any means, electronic, mechanical, photocopying, or
otherwise, without the prior permission of the publisher.

A CIP catalog record for this book is available from the
Library of Congress and the British Library.

ISBN: 978 1 78249 148 4

Printed in China

Editor: Clare Sayer
Designer: Vicky Rankin
Photographer: Gavin Kingcome
Stylists: Nel Haynes and Jo Thornhill
Illustrator: Harriet de Winton

In-house designer: Fahema Khanam
Art director: Sally Powell
Production manager: Gordana Simacovic
Publishing manager: Penny Craig
Publisher: Cindy Richards

Waltham Forest Libraries

904 000 00415088	
Askews & Holts	05-Dec-2014
746.13 GOU	£14.99
4503600	☺

Notes

For most of the projects you will need a **basic sewing kit** of
scissors, needles, pins, tape measure, and sewing thread.

CICO Books have made every effort to provide safe and accurate
instructions for the projects in this book. However, the publisher
cannot accept liability for injuries or property damage that might
occur from attempting to make the projects.

Always take care when handling dye and other chemicals, and
keep them out of reach of children and animals.

Contents

Techniques

Indigo is extracted from the leaves of the plant *Indigofera tinctoria*, and has been used for centuries to dye all kinds of fabric a rich, vibrant blue. From its origins as a naturally produced dye, most common in India, to its ubiquitous appearance in blue jeans today, indigo has traveled far and wide.

Dyeing with indigo

Indigo extract is available in the form of a powder that is easily obtained from craft and dye stores, some of which are listed on page 142.

During the dyeing process indigo powder is used along with the minerals spectralite and soda ash, also available from craft and dye stores. These chemicals should all be used with care, and stored away from and out of reach of children and pets. Be sure to wear rubber gloves when using these materials, and wash your hands after handling them.

Spectralite removes the oxygen present in water. Once the oxygen is no longer present, the indigo powder will dissolve. We then add a soda ash solution in small amounts at a time in order to alter the pH level. The soda ash raises the pH: to dye animal fibers like wool or silk we need it to be ph9; for plant fibers such as cotton or linen we need it to be ph11.

Use only old utensils and pots that will never be used for food preparation again. And as indigo is very strong, keep the pan you use just for indigo, do not use it for other dyes.

Indigo dyeing is also quite messy so you will need an apron and it is best to dye outside if possible. Along with the usual warnings about using dyes, there is one other: beware, indigo dyeing is addictive!

Indigo dyeing requires the use of two vats or containers, one large and one smaller. The smaller one is used for the preparation of the indigo solution; a large glass jar with a lid is ideal for this, as you can see what is going on and keep the solution covered. The larger vat is the one you will actually dip your fabrics into, and a large old saucepan is useful for this.

As you dye with indigo, it is very important to avoid introducing oxygen into the dye vat. It is possible to minimize this by sliding the fabric carefully down one side of the vat without disturbing the surface. Where an even finish is required, the fibers can be "worked" under the surface with your fingers for a few moments. When removing the fabric from the vat, leave a tail of fabric in the vat through which excess dye can dribble back into the vat. This is also done at the side of the vat, to prevent splashing which would introduce oxygen into the vat.

Once you have finished dyeing, there are a few things to remember about storing dye solutions. Soda ash solution can be stored in plastic bottles for future use. Label well and store away from pets and children. An indigo vat that still has dye present can also be covered and saved to be revived at a later date. It can be revived by adding a teaspoonful of spectralite and warming; after an hour, a blue metallic layer will be on the surface and it will be ready to use.

A safe and fun way to dispose of a used vat is to add shredded newspaper to the liquid until it is all soaked up, and then use the paper pulp for sculpting or paper-making.

Preparing the indigo vat

You will need

- 1 oz (25 g) indigo powder— this will dye 4½ lb (2 kg) of fiber or fabric
- Spectralite
- 1¼ pt (600 ml) warm water
- Large glass jar with a screw-top lid
- Teaspoon
- 5¼ oz (150 g) soda ash
- Jug
- Litmus paper (to test pH level)
- Large pan with a lid

1 Place the indigo powder in the glass jar with 3 teaspoons (15 ml) of spectralite and a little of the warm water. Stir well to make a paste, then mix in ½ pt (200 ml) of the warm water.

2 Add the soda ash to the rest of the warm water in a jug and stir well. Add the soda ash solution to the indigo solution a little at a time, using the litmus paper to check the pH level after each addition. Stop adding the soda solution when the desired pH is reached (see the note on fibers on page 7).

3 Cover the jar by placing the lid on loosely, and set it aside in a warm place for the solution to develop (it must be kept warm for this to happen). This will take 30–40 minutes. While this is happening, prepare the large vat by filling a large pan two-thirds full with warm water and adding 1 tsp (5 ml) of spectralite to it. Keep this pan covered and warm.

_4_ The indigo solution in the jar is ready when you can see both a metallic blue layer on the surface and a yellow liquid beneath. This is due to the dye on the surface of the vat reacting with oxygen in the air; the liquid below remains yellow because it is not in contact with any oxygen.

_5_ Add the indigo solution to the spectralite solution in the large vat by lowering the jar into the vat; do not pour the indigo solution in, as pouring could cause splashing, which would introduce oxygen into the vat.

_6_ Leave the vat covered and warm for an hour. It is ready to use when the surface of the vat is covered in metallic blue bubbles with an oily appearance.

chapter 1
plain and dip-dyeing

If you are new to dyeing, then plain dyeing (simply dyeing a whole piece of fabric) will help you master the technique of preparing the indigo vat, and become familiar with the effect of the dye on different fabrics. Dip-dyeing, where only part of the fabric is dipped into the vat, with less being dipped each time, is another simple technique for beginners to try.

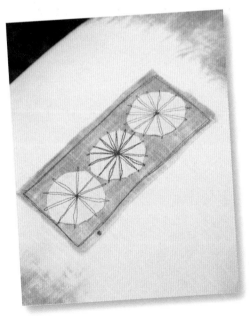

plain and dip-dyeing techniques

Plain dyeing is, by its nature, the most straightforward technique. The fabric is immersed in a prepared indigo vat for just a few seconds, then rinsed several times, washed, and dried to produce a piece of plain blue fabric. Dip-dyeing produces different results, as you can vary the shade of indigo by building up layers, airing, and allowing the dye to develop each time before repeating the dipping process. Because items only need to be dipped into the indigo vat for a few moments, an attractive graded effect can be achieved easily and quickly, with the color ranging from light blue to darkest indigo.

You will need

- Fabric
- Prepared indigo vat (see page 8)
- Rubber gloves and apron
- Bowls for soaking and rinsing
- White household vinegar
- Washing detergent

To plain dye

1 Soak the fabric in clean, cold water for a couple of hours to prevent air pockets forming. (If oxygen is present, the dye won't work.) Remove from the bowl and gently squeeze out all the excess water.

2 Immerse all of the fabric in the dye vat for a few seconds, taking care to disturb the surface of the dye solution as little as possible by sliding the fabric in down the side of the vat. Work the fibers under the surface with your fingers in order to get an even result.

3 Remove the fabric from the solution slowly, at the side of the vat, leaving a tail of fabric in the vat through which excess dye can dribble gently back into it. Air the fabric to develop the color—this can happen very quickly! You can either hold the fabric or, for larger pieces, drape them over a washing line. It is best to do this outdoors, because dye solution will drip from the fabric. If you want a darker shade, dip the fabric in the vat again for a few seconds, as above, and air the fabric again. Continue to dip and air until you are happy with the shade.

4 Rinse the fabric in several changes of cold water, until dye no longer comes out of the fabric. Rinse once more, adding white household vinegar to the final rinse. You will need about ¼ pt (100 ml) of vinegar per 2 pt (1 l) of water in the final rinse. This neutralizes the pH, to prevent damage to the fabric. Wash with detergent and hang the fabric out to dry.

To dip dye

1 Soak the fabric in clean, cold water for a couple of hours to prevent air pockets from forming. (If oxygen is present, the dye won't work.) Remove from the bowl and gently squeeze out all the excess water.

2 Dip a portion of the fabric into the dye vat, aiming to disturb the surface as little as possible by sliding the fabric in down the side of the vat. This first portion will be the total extent of the dip-dyed area. Work the fibers under the surface with your fingers in order to get an even result.

3 Remove the fabric from the solution slowly at the side of the vat, leaving a tail of fabric in the vat through which excess dye can dribble gently back into it. Air the fabric to develop the color, either by holding the fabric or, for larger pieces, by draping them over a washing line. It is best to do this outdoors, because dye solution will drip from the fabric.

4 Repeat the dipping process several times, leaving a little more of the fabric out of the vat each time. This way a gradual darkening effect can be achieved, with the end of the fabric that is dipped most often being the darkest blue.

5 Rinse the fabric in several changes of cold water, until dye no longer comes out of the fabric. Rinse once more, adding white household vinegar to the final rinse. You will need about ¼ pt (100 ml) of vinegar per 2 pt (1 l) of water in the final rinse. This neutralizes the pH, to prevent damage to the fabric. Wash with detergent and hang the fabric out to dry.

appliquéd
needlecase

Combine some old woolen blanket dyed a deep indigo blue as a result of repeated dippings with some that is in its undyed state to make a useful addition to your sewing kit. Decorated with simple embroidery, scraps of old fabric, and notions, this pretty little case will keep your needles safe and close to hand.

You will need

- Prepared indigo vat (see page 8)
- Rubber gloves and apron
- Bowls for soaking and rinsing
- White household vinegar
- Washing detergent
- Outer fabric: 7 x 4½ in. (18 x 11 cm) wool blanket or wool felt
- Inner fabric: 5½ x 3¼ in. (12.5 x 8.2 cm) undyed wool blanket or wool felt
- Embroidery floss (thread) and needle
- Scraps of pretty fabrics
- Buttons and/or trimmings
- Old cloth tape measure or ribbon, 6 in. (15 cm) long
- Basic sewing kit
- Sewing machine

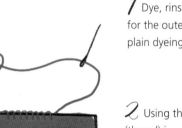

1 Dye, rinse, and wash the wool blanket or felt for the outer fabric, following the instructions for plain dyeing on pages 13–14. Allow to dry.

2 Using three strands of embroidery floss (thread) in a contrast color, stitch around your piece of dyed wool fabric, using blanket stitch (see page 138). Start stitching at the center of one of the long sides for a neat finish. Repeat this step for the undyed piece of wool fabric.

3 Embellish one side of the cover of your needle case with scraps of fabric and buttons. Here a simple flower shape is created by hand stitching petal-shaped scraps around a button, using embroidery floss and a running stitch.

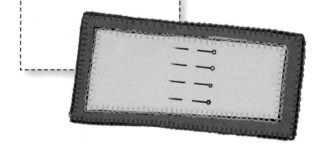

4 Assemble the needlecase by positioning the undyed piece of wool fabric in the center of the outer cover, on the wrong side. Pin or baste (tack) in place. Turn the needlecase over so that the cover is facing up.

5 Place the tape measure or ribbon in place to form the spine of the needlecase. Tuck the ends under at the top and bottom and then pin or baste in place. Machine stitch along each side of the tape measure or ribbon.

dip-dyed
pashmina shawl

The beauty of indigo and the many shades of blue it can produce can be seen in this project. Any woolen shawl or scarf can be used, with the shading producing a very attractive effect.

You will need

- Pashmina or fine woolen shawl
- Prepared indigo vat (see page 8)
- Rubber gloves and apron
- Bowls for soaking and rinsing
- White household vinegar
- Washing detergent

1 Soak the shawl in clean cold water for a couple of hours.

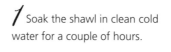

2 Squeeze out all the excess water and then fold the shawl in half and hold it up so that both fringed ends are hanging down—another pair of hands will make this easier! Wearing rubber gloves, dip the shawl into the indigo vat so that both ends are immersed, with the center section of the shawl above the surface.

3 Repeat the dipping process, this time leaving a little more of the shawl above the surface of the dye. Keep dipping in this way, airing the shawl between dips, until the very ends of the shawl are the desired shade. You may need to dip four or five times to get the gradation of color you want.

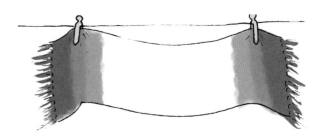

4 Rinse carefully in several changes of cold water until no excess dye remains. Add white vinegar to the final rinse and then wash with detergent. Allow to dry, then press on the correct setting.

dip-dyed
bench pillow

Crisp linen, folded and dipped into the indigo vat and then finished with a freemotion machine-embroidered motif, makes a lovely addition to a garden bench. Here's a simple way to make a zipped pillow with a tidy finish.

You will need

- Prepared indigo vat (see page 8)
- Rubber gloves and apron
- Bowls for soaking and rinsing
- White household vinegar
- Washing detergent
- Two pieces of linen, each measuring 27 x 17 in. (67.5 x 42.5 cm)
- Embellishments such as appliqué or embroidery (optional)
- 27-in. (67.5-cm) zipper
- Pillow form (cushion pad) to fit
- Basic sewing kit
- Sewing machine

1 Soak the linen fabric in clean, cold water for a couple of hours.

2 Remove from the bowl and squeeze out any excess water, then dip-dye the short ends of both pieces of linen, following the instructions on pages 14–15. Make sure you fold the linen in half across its width to dye the two short ends evenly. Rinse, wash, and leave to dry.

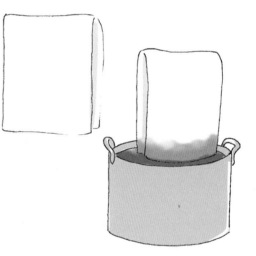

3 Once the two dyed pieces are completely dry, press them and add any embellishments to the front, such as appliqué or embroidery, if desired.

4 With right sides together, pin and machine stitch the long side of one of the pieces of linen to one side of the zipper. Repeat with the other piece of linen and the other side of the zipper. Zigzag through both the linen and the edge of the zipper tape to prevent fraying.

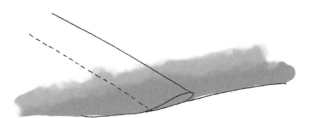

5 With the right sides uppermost and the zipper lying horizontally, create a small overlap to conceal the zipper. Pin in place and then machine stitch, using the zipper foot on your sewing machine and following the teeth of the zipper to give a neat finish. Open the zipper.

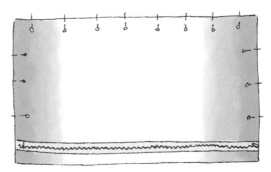

6 Pin the remaining three sides right sides together, with the zipper lying flat to one side. Machine stitch around the edges, taking a ¾-in. (2-cm) seam allowance.

7 Snip the corners to reduce bulk and and zigzag stitch around the seams to neaten. Turn the cover right side out and insert the pillow form (cushion pad).

dip-dyed *lampshade*

Silk is a lovely fabric to work with and indigo works so well with it! Repeated graded dipping can give you a gradual darkening of the shade of blue achieved which produces an attractive finish.

You will need

- Prepared indigo vat (see page 8)
- Rubber gloves and apron
- Bowls for soaking and rinsing
- White household vinegar
- Washing detergent
- Enough plain silk fabric to make one lampshade (refer to your lampshade kit for guidance)
- Drum lampshade kit (see suppliers on page 143)

1 Soak the silk fabric in clean, cold water for a couple of hours.

2 Remove from the bowl and squeeze out any excess water. Fold the fabric in half widthways and dip-dye one end of the fabric, following the instructions on pages 14–15.

3 Repeat the dipping process, each time leaving a little more of the fabric out of the vat. This way you will achieve a gradual color change.

4 Rinse carefully in several changes of cold water until no excess dye remains. Add vinegar to the final rinse and then wash with detergent. Allow to dry on the line and then press the fabric carefully.

chapter 2
batik printing

Batik printing is one of the oldest methods for making patterns in dyed fabrics, and is most commonly associated with the island of Java in Indonesia. By coating parts of the fabric with wax before dyeing, you can create beautiful and ornate patterns, because the fabric covered in wax remains undyed.

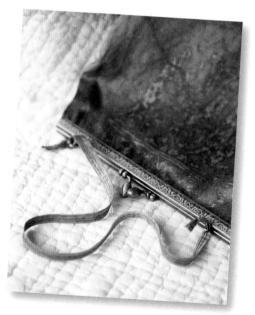

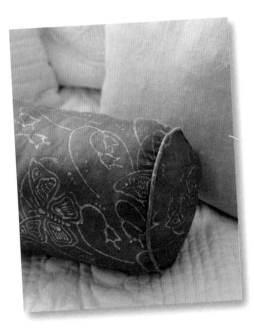

batik printing Techniques

Printing with cold liquid batik wax is a method that can produce some really beautiful, elegant fabrics in indigo. It uses wooden printing blocks or patterned rollers to transfer a design in wax onto the fabric, thereby masking out areas that will be left undyed. In both cases cold liquid batik wax is applied to the fabric and left to set, then the fabric is dyed, rinsed, washed, and dried as usual. If you are using wooden printing blocks, the wax is painted on with an ordinary paintbrush and then the block is placed on the fabric. Patterned rollers work with a paint applicator, which is filled with cold liquid batik wax instead of paint.

To print with a roller

You will need
- Fabric
- Cold liquid batik wax (see Suppliers and Resources, page 142)
- Prepared indigo vat (see page 8)
- Bowls for soaking and rinsing
- White household vinegar
- Washing detergent
- A wooden printing block, or patterned roller with applicator system (see Suppliers and Resources, page 142)
- Paintbrush (for block printing only)
- Paper towels
- Iron

1 Fill the reservoir section of the applicator system with cold liquid batik wax and then position the roller in the frame, which forms the handle of the roller.

2 Hang your fabric on a firm, flat, vertical surface—a wall or the back of a door is ideal. Draw the roller down the length of the fabric.

3 Repeat, moving across the fabric. Work quickly and carefully, lining up the pattern each time.

4 As it dries, the liquid batik wax will turn from white (when liquid) to a waxy yellow.

5 Once the wax has dried, soak the fabric in cold water for a couple of hours, then remove from the bowl, and gently squeeze out any excess water, taking care not to damage the wax. Follow the instructions for plain dyeing on pages 13–14 to dye and rinse the prepared fabric, but only dip the fabric in the vat once, as the wax will not survive repeated dippings.

6 Scrape off any excess wax, then wash with detergent and allow to dry. Most of the wax will come out when the fabric is washed, but remove any wax still remaining by laying paper towels over the fabric and pressing gently with a cool iron. The wax will metl and be absorbed into the paper.

To print with a wooden block

1 Paint the cold liquid batik wax onto the printing block with a paintbrush.

2 Press the block down onto your prepared fabric. Remove the block and leave the wax to dry.

3 Once the wax has dried, soak the fabric in cold water for a couple of hours, then remove from the bowl, and gently squeeze out any excess water, taking care not to damage the wax. Follow the instructions for plain dyeing on pages 13–14 to dye and rinse the prepared fabric, but only dip the fabric once as the wax will not survive repeated dippings. Scrape off any excess wax, then wash with detergent and allow to dry. Remove any remaining wax by laying paper towels over the fabric and pressing gently with a cool iron. The wax will melt and be absorbed into the paper.

vintage-style
frame bag

Solid wooden Indian blocks print well with cold liquid batik wax. Printing on silk gives a wonderful, glamorous effect and a metal framed purse is always a joy to use!

You will need

- Cold liquid batik wax
- Printing block
- Paintbrush
- Approximately 10 in. (25 cm) white silk fabric, 36 in. (90 cm) wide, for the outer bag
- Prepared indigo vat (see page 8)
- Rubber gloves and apron
- Bowls for soaking and rinsing
- White household vinegar
- Washing detergent
- Paper towels
- Iron
- Sew-in purse (bag) frame (the type with holes), 8 in. (20 cm) wide
- Plain paper to make a pattern
- Approximately 10 in. (25 cm) contrast fabric, 36 in. (90 cm) wide, for the lining
- Basic sewing kit
- Sewing machine

1 First decorate the silk for the outer bag, using a printing block and following the instructions on page 37. Wash as instructed, allow to dry, remove any excess wax with a cool iron and paper towels, and then press flat.

2 Place your bag frame on the plain paper. Mark the center of the frame and draw around the outside of it. Measure from the top of the frame down to the hinge and make a note of this measurement.

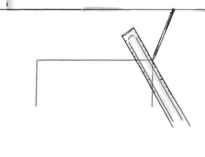

3 Using a ruler and pencil, mark out a line down from the top corner of one side of the bag frame at roughly a 30-degree angle and the length of your noted measurement, adding ½ in. (1 cm) for ease; this is where the hinges will sit in the finished bag's opening. Mark this spot carefully.

4 Working on one side of the bag pattern only, draw out the shape of your bag, curving the base slightly. Once you are happy with the shape, fold the paper in half at the point where you marked the center point of the frame. Cut out the pattern with the paper still folded, working carefully in order to make a symmetrical shape.

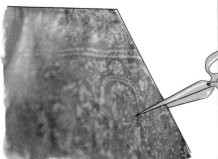

5 Using the pattern you have just make, cut out two pattern pieces from the bag's outer fabric and two from the contrast lining fabric. Cut a ½-in. (1-cm) slit where you have marked the hinge opening—this must be done accurately!

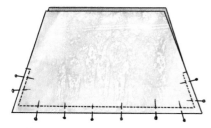

6 Place the two outer bag pieces right sides together, line up the slits, and pin down from the slit on one side, across the bottom, and up to the slit on the other side. Machine stitch, taking a ½-in. (1-cm) seam allowance. Repeat with the lining fabric, pinning carefully so that the openings will all line up.

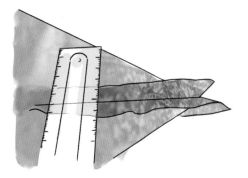

7 With both the "bags" still inside out, press the seams open. Place your hand in the corners of each bag and line the opened seams up with one another to create a boxed base. Once flat, use a ruler to mark a line across this seam, 1 in. (2.5 cm) from the corner, ensuring that both lines are the same distance from the corners. Machine stitch across each of the lines and then cut off the corner, trimming the excess neatly back to ½ in. (1 cm).

8 Turn the lining bag right side out and place it inside the outer bag, which is still inside out at this point; the two bags will now be right sides together. Put your hands in each of the boxed corners to help line up the opening of the bag.

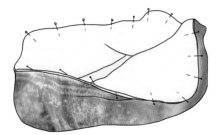

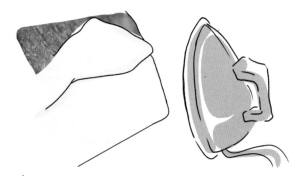

9 Working from where each of the hinges will sit, carefully pin the inner and outer parts of your bag together; this will form the opening. Ease in any fabric that doesn't quite match up.

10 Stitch all around the opening taking a ½-in. (1-cm) seam allowance, working carefully and removing pins as you do so. Using a stitch ripper, make an opening in what will be the inside base of the bag (the lining)—it needs to be just large enough to get your hand in, approximately 3–4 in. (8–10 cm). Turn the entire bag right side out through this hole, easing out the seams as you do so. Use an iron to press the seams flat if needed. Close the hole you made either by stitching it closed by hand or using a sewing machine; this stitching will not be seen!

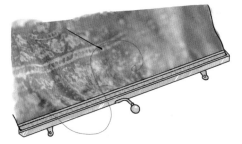

11 Using a very strong thread, stitch the finished bag firmly onto the frame, keeping your stitches as neat and even as possible. I used backstitch (see page 137) for added strength.

12 To make the strap, cut a strip of fabric approximately 1 in. (2.5 cm) wide. Fold it in half lengthwise, with wrong sides together, and press. Open out, then fold each long raw edge in to the center crease. Fold along the center crease again, then topstitch down the strap, through all four layers. Knot the finished strap securely to the frame.

Three-fold
room divider

Screens are always a glamorous addition to any room and a lovely way to use patterned indigo in a room. Any pattern would work with this project, and you can get the MDF cut to size at your local hardware or home improvement store.

You will need

- Patterned roller and applicator system (I used No. 12 roller from The Painted House; see Suppliers, page 142)
- Cold liquid batik wax
- Six pieces of fabric, ideally with a twill or satin surface, each measuring 75 x 25 in. (187.5 x 62.5 cm)
- Prepared indigo vat (see page 8)
- Rubber gloves and apron
- Bowls for soaking and rinsing
- White household vinegar
- Washing detergent
- Paper towels
- Iron
- Three pieces of MDF, each measuring 68 x 18 x ⅝ in. (170 x 45 x 1.5 cm)
- Staple gun
- Six 1½ in. (4 cm) brass butt hinges and screws
- PVA glue
- 15 yds (13 m) braid or cotton tape, ⅝ in (1.5 cm) wide

1 Fill the reservoir of the applicator system with cold liquid batik wax and position the roller in the frame.

2 Pin the fabric panels to a vertical surface and print your pattern (see pages 34–35). Leave the wax to dry.

3 Soak, dye, and rinse the fabric panels, following the instructions on page 36. Scrape off any excess wax, then wash with detergent and allow to dry.

4 To remove any remaining wax sitting on the surface of the fabric, place absorbent paper towels over the fabric and press gently with a cool iron. The wax will melt and be absorbed into the paper.

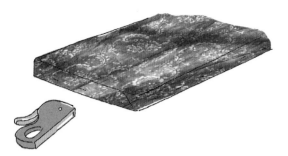

5 Using the staple gun, attach the fabric to the edge of the MDF sheets. Staple down one side first and then pull the fabric tightly to the other side, smoothing the fabric as you work and folding the corners in neatly. Continue until all sides of all the panels are covered and trim away any excess fabric after stapling.

6 Place one side of the first set of hinges at intervals along one edge of the first panel, and attach securely with screws—these will be covered with braid or tape later.

7 Use PVA glue to attach the braid or tape over the stapled edges, starting and finishing at the center of the edge that will stand on the floor. Use additional staples if necessary to secure the braid along this edge as they will not be seen.

8 Place the second panel on top of the first panel and line up the edges before attaching the other side of the hinges with screws.

9 Attach one side of the second set of hinges to the opposite edge of the second panel. Glue and staple braid or tape as before, covering the screws and hinges on the second panel.

10 Place the third panel on top, taking care to line it up accurately. Attach the other sides of the hinges with screws and cover the edges with tape or braid as before.

easy *roman shade*

This is a really simple way to make a shade that has no need for rods, and allows the light to shine through the batik pattern. Using patterned rollers and cold liquid batik wax, which is simple to remove, is a quick way to produce something for your home that is both beautiful and unique!

1 Fill the reservoir of the applicator system with cold liquid batik wax and position the roller in the frame. Pin the fabric to a vertical surface and print your pattern (see pages 34–35). Leave the wax to dry. Soak, dye, and rinse the fabric, following the instructions on page 36. Scrape off any excess wax, then wash with detergent.
Leave to dry, then place paper towels over the fabric and press gently with a cool iron to remove any remaining wax.

2 Fold over and hem both sides of the fabric, using a double 1-in. (2.5-cm) hem. Turn up a double 2-in. (5-cm) hem along the bottom and stitch close to the fold to form a channel for the lower batten—both ends of the channel need to be open. Check your desired drop again and turn over the top edge to this measurement. Press. Cut a piece of hook-and-loop tape to the width of your shade and stitch the loop (soft) side to the top of the shade.

You will need

- Patterned roller and applicator system (I used Tuvi roller, from The Painted House; see Suppliers, page 142)
- Cold liquid batik wax
- Plain fabric (see Calculating fabric, below), pre-washed and dried
- Prepared indigo vat (see page 8)
- Rubber gloves and apron
- Bowls for soaking and rinsing
- White household vinegar
- Washing detergent
- Paper towels
- Iron
- Basic sewing kit
- Sewing machine
- Two pieces of ¼ x 1-in. (0.5 x 2.5-cm) wooden batten, the width of your finished shade minus 2 in. (5 cm)
- Hook-and-loop tape
- Small brass rings
- Cord
- Screw eyes
- 1 x 1 in. (2.5 x 2.5 cm) wooden batten
- Drill
- Cleat for the cord

Calculating Fabric

To calculate how much fabric you need, work out how long and wide you want the finished shade to be; it's up to you whether you hang the shade on the inside or the outside of the window recess. Add 4 in. (10 cm) to both the width and the length, to allow for the hems.

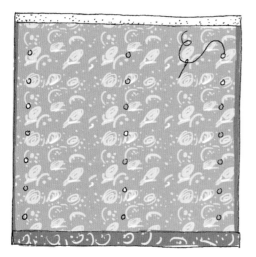

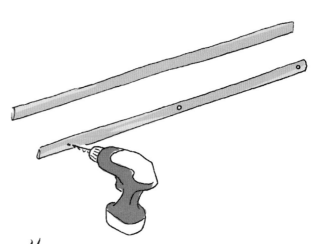

3 In order to work out how many brass rings you need, you will need to decide how many folds you would like in the shade when it is pulled up—they should be evenly spaced and can be anything from 6–10 in. (15–25 cm) apart. Each fold will need three rings—one at each side and one in the center (for very wide shades you may need another line of rings). Pin and stitch the rings in place according to your calculations.

4 Mark and drill one of the pieces of thin wooden batten so that the holes line up with the rings on the shade. Slip the undrilled piece into the stitched channel at the bottom of the shade.

5 Take three pieces of cord and tie them through the holes that you have drilled in the thin wooden batten. Then thread them vertically up through the rings on the shade.

6 Fix the three screw eyes into the underside of the 1 x 1 in. (2.5 x 2.5 cm) wooden batten so that they line up with the rings on the shade. Fix the batten in place on the wall or window frame and then staple the hook (stiff) side of the hook-and-loop tape to the front of the batten. Attach the shade to the batten using the hook-and-loop tape and then pass the cords through the screw eyes. Arrange so that the cords are even, knot firmly, and trim the ends. Fix the cleat to the wall or window frame, and loop the cords around it.

butterfly
bolster pillow

Bolster cushions are always a welcoming addition to a sofa or armchair, tucking in just where you need them. This one is simple to make using a slipstitch to close, with no need of a zipped opening.

You will need

- Patterned roller and fabric applicator system (I used No. 14 roller from The Painted House; see Suppliers, page 142)
- Cold liquid batik wax
- 1 yd (90 cm) fabric, 36 in. (90 cm) wide, pre-washed and dried
- Prepared indigo vat (see page 8)
- Rubber gloves and apron
- Bowls for soaking and rinsing
- White household vinegar
- Washing detergent
- Paper towels
- Iron
- 1½ yds (1.3 m) piping cord, cut into two
- Sewing machine
- Basic sewing kit
- Bolster pillow form (cushion pad), approximately 6 x 18 in. (15 x 45 cm)

1 Fill the reservoir of the applicator system with cold liquid batik wax and position the roller in the frame. Pin the fabric to a vertical surface and print your pattern (see pages 34–35). Leave the wax to dry. Soak, dye, and rinse the fabric, following the instructions on page 36. Scrape off any excess wax, then wash with detergent. Leave to dry, then place paper towels over the fabric and press gently with a cool iron to remove any remaining wax.

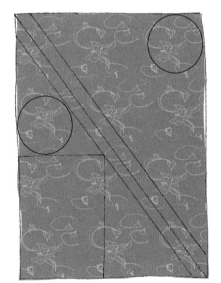

2 Lay your fabric out flat. Using the diagram as a guide, cut out the following pieces: one rectangle measuring 20 x 18 in. (50 x 45 cm), two circles measuring 6 in. (15 cm) in diameter, and two strips of fabric on the bias, each approximately 1¼ in. (4 cm) wide.

3 Using the piping or zipper foot on your sewing machine, use the strips of bias-cut fabric to cover both pieces of piping cord (see page 136). There should be no need to join strips.

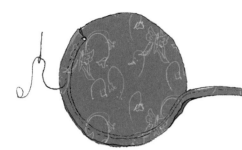

4 Stitch the prepared piping onto the circles, using a sewing machine with a piping foot (or backstitch by hand—see page 137). Start and finish at the center bottom of each circle, folding and overlapping the fabric for a neat join (see page 136).

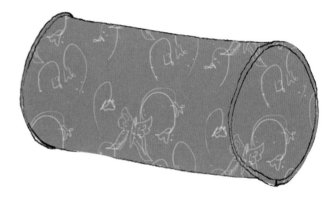

5 With right sides together, pin and stitch the longest sides of the rectangular piece to the piped circles, again starting and finishing at the center bottom. Leave a few inches either side of the join unstitched; this will be stitched later.

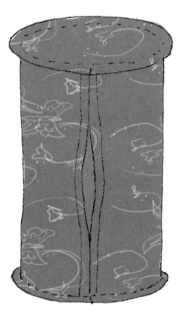

6 Change the foot on your sewing machine to a presser foot and stitch together the long vertical seam that sits at the bottom of the bolster using a straight stitch. Leave a gap of around 6 in. (15 cm) through which you can insert the pillow form (cushion pad) later. Gently press the seam open. Stitch closed the circular ends, trimming away any waste fabric.

7 Turn the cover right side out before inserting the pillow form. Pin and slipstitch the opening closed (see page 138).

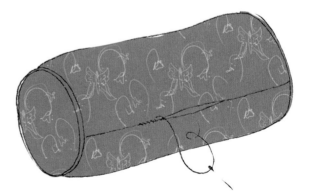

Seed-head *apron*

Plain cotton drill aprons are easily found and just as easily printed and dyed. Using a fresh indigo vat gives a very dark indigo blue, which shows off the attractive pattern well!

You will need

- Patterned roller and fabric applicator system (I used Tussock roller from The Painted House; see Suppliers, page 142)
- Cold liquid batik wax
- Plain cotton drill apron in white, cream, or ecru
- Prepared indigo vat (see page 8)
- Rubber gloves and apron
- Bowls for soaking and rinsing
- White household vinegar
- Washing detergent
- Paper towels
- Iron

1 Fill the reservoir of the applicator system with cold liquid batik wax and position the roller in the frame. Pin the apron to a vertical surface and print the lower half of the apron (see pages 34–24). Leave the wax to dry.

2 Soak and dye the apron, following the instructions on page 36.

3 Rinse well, adding white vinegar to the final rinse. Scrape off any excess wax, then wash in detergent, and allow the apron to dry.

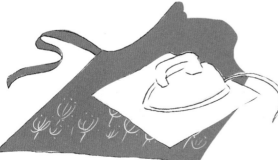

4 Once the apron in completely dry, place sheets of absorbent paper towel over the fabric and press gently with a cool iron. Any remaining wax will melt and be absorbed into the paper.

batik stenciling

The beauty of batik dyeing is that the undyed areas let light through in quite a magical way. We've already looked at batik printing, but if you want to create larger undyed areas, then stenciling is another option. You can easily create your own stencil patterns by tracing patterns you like from fabric or from photographs or drawings, but we have provided templates for the projects in this chapter, if you want to recreate the same design.

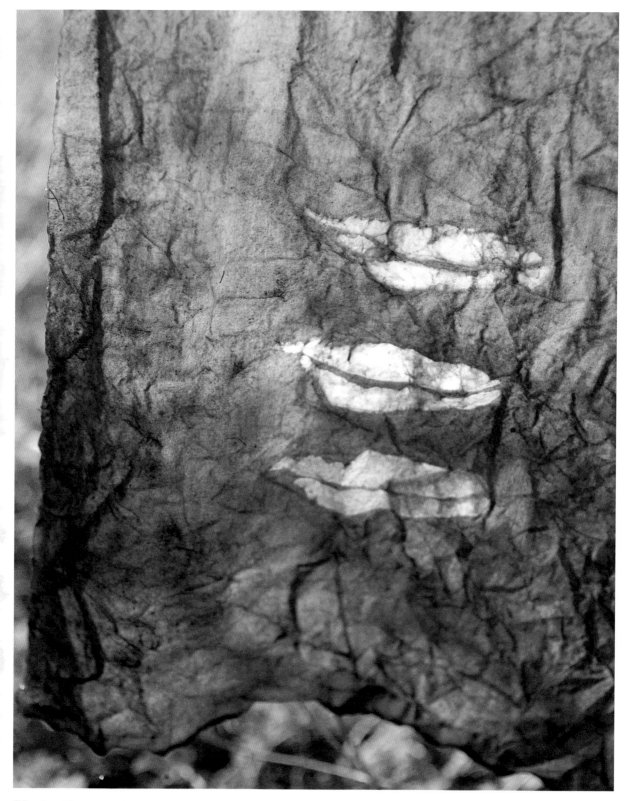

batik stenciling Techniques

Applying wax to fabric using a stencil is another excellent way of creating patterns. Batik stenciling is traditionally done using beeswax, but I prefer to use soya wax, which melts at a much lower temperature, and is easier to remove by washing, and ironing through paper towels if necessary. This is a lot safer than some of the methods employed to remove beeswax, which involve solvents. Because the indigo vat is kept warm rather than hot, the soya wax won't melt during the dyeing process. You can use ready-made stencils or cut your own, for something truly individual. Shiny card works well for stencil, and if you don't have a craft knife then a very sharp pair of small scissors will do.

You will need

- Template
- Tracing or greaseproof paper
- Pencil
- Shiny card
- Craft knife or sharp scissors
- Soya wax flakes
- Double boiler or microwave
- Fabric
- Sponge applicator
- Prepared indigo vat (see page 8)
- Rubber gloves and apron
- Bowls for soaking and rinsing
- White household vinegar
- Washing detergent
- Paper towels
- Iron

1 Trace the template or other design onto the tracing or greaseproof paper using a pencil. Turn the paper over and draw over the reverse side in pencil.

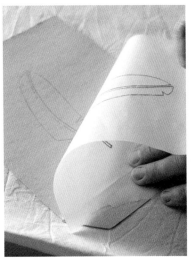

2 Transfer the image onto a piece of shiny card by placing the image face down and going over the pencil lines on the reverse again. The outline of the design will be transferred onto the card.

3 Cut out the shape with a craft knife or a pair of sharp scissors.

4 Melt the wax in a double boiler on the hob or place it in a glass container and heat it in a microwave in 30-second bursts, until it is completely liquid. It is important not to overheat the wax.

5 Protect your work surface with old newspapers. Place the stencil on your fabric and, working quickly, use the sponge applicator to apply the wax through the stencil. The wax will need to soak through the fabric before it sets. Don't worry about blobs of wax or areas where the edges aren't perfect, as this is all part of the charm and attractiveness of batik stenciling.

6 Once the wax is dry, soak the fabric in tepid (not cold) water for a couple of hours. If the water is too cold, the soya wax may crack. Remove the fabric and squeeze out any excess water, taking great care not to damage the wax.

7 Dye and rinse the fabric (see pages 13–14), but only dip the fabric in the vat once, as the wax will not survive repeated dippings. Scrape off any excess wax, then wash with detergent and allow to dry. Lay paper towels over the fabric and press with a cool iron to remove any remaining wax.

leaf *curtain*

Voile curtains with a simple motif repeated along the hem are a charming way to decorate a window. Leaf shapes work well with batik.

You will need

- Leaf template (see page 139)
- Tracing or greaseproof paper
- Pencil
- Shiny card
- Sharp scissors or craft knife
- 2–4 oz (50–100 g) soya wax flakes
- Double boiler
- Old newspapers
- Ready-made voile curtain, pre-washed and dried
- Brush or sponge applicator
- Prepared indigo vat (see page 8)
- Rubber gloves and apron
- Bowls for soaking and rinsing
- White household vinegar
- Washing detergent
- Paper towels
- Iron

1 Trace the leaf template on page 139 onto shiny card and cut out your stencil (see pages 55–56).

2 Melt the wax in a double boiler on the hob or place in a glass container and heat in a microwave in 30-second bursts (see page 56).

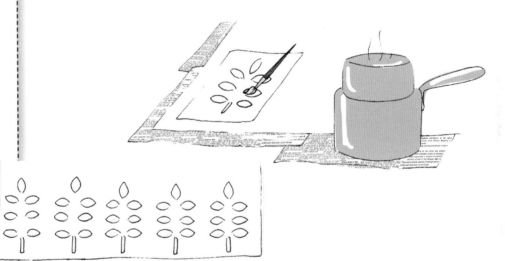

3 Protect your work surface with old newspapers, as the wax will go through the fabric and it can get a little messy! Place the stencil on the bottom left corner of the fabric and apply the wax over the top, using either a brush or sponge applicator. Repeat along the bottom of the fabric and then allow the wax to cool and harden.

4 Once the wax has set, briefly soak the fabric in tepid water to remove any oxygen bubbles that may be trapped in the dry fiber (cold water will crack the wax).

5 Squeeze out the excess water, being careful to avoid spoiling the wax, and dye and rinse in the usual way, remembering to add vinegar to the final rinse (see pages 13–14).

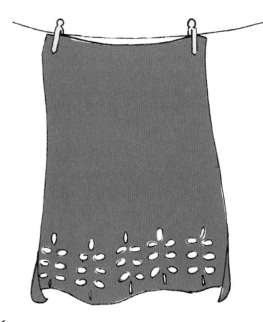

6 Scrape as much of the wax off as possible then wash the voile in very hot water and washing detergent. This should remove most, if not all, of the remaining wax. Allow to dry.

7 If there are any traces of wax remaining on the voile it can be removed by placing the voile between two pieces of paper towel and using a hot iron. Repeat with new paper each time until there is no more residue coming through onto the paper.

feather stenciled
Tablet cover

We still use paper notebooks as well as electronic devices—this cover will fit both! Use the batik stencil method to reproduce the image of a feather for the front cover. Simple measuring instructions mean that you can make this cover to fit any size of device.

You will need

- Feather template (see page 141)
- Tracing or greaseproof paper
- Pencil
- Shiny card
- Sharp scissors or craft knife
- 2 oz (50 g) soya wax flakes
- Double boiler or microwave
- Old newspapers
- Piece of calico twelve times the size of your device
- Sponge applicator
- Prepared indigo vat (see page 8)
- Rubber gloves and apron
- Bowls for soaking and rinsing
- White household vinegar
- Washing detergent
- Iron and paper towels
- Basic sewing kit
- 2 in. (5 cm) hook-and-loop tape
- 18 in. (45 cm) elastic, ¼ in. (5 mm) wide, cut into four pieces
- Two pieces of corrugated card the same size as your device

1 Trace the feather template on page 141 onto shiny card and cut out your stencil (see pages 55–56).

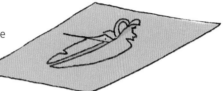

2 Melt the wax in a double boiler on the hob or place in a glass container and heat in a microwave in 30-second bursts—it is important not to overheat the wax (see page 56).

3 Cut off a piece of calico: it needs to be three and a half times the width plus 2 in. (5 cm) by the depth of your device plus 2 in. (5 cm).

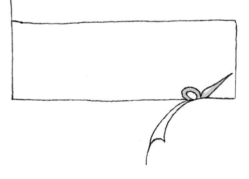

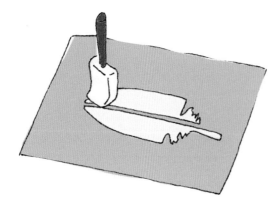

4 Protect your work surface with old newspapers. Position your feather stencil over the fabric and, working on one end of the fabric only, use a sponge applicator to apply the melted wax through the cut-out stencil. Work quite quickly, as the wax will need to go right through the fabric before setting. Repeat to create a design of three feathers. Leave the wax to cool and harden.

5 When the wax is dry, soak the fabric in clean, tepid water for a couple of hours and then squeeze out the excess water. Dye and rinse, following the instructions on pages 13–14. Scrape off as much of the wax as possible with the blade of a knife, then wash in detergent and dry. Remove any remaining wax by laying paper towels over the fabric and pressing with a cool iron.

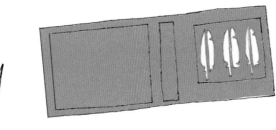

6 Cut the following pieces from the dyed fabric: the first (with the feather motif) should be the same size as your device, the second (for the tab) needs to be 4 x 4 in. (10 x 10 cm), and the final piece should be the same height and twice the width of your device plus 1 in. (2.5 cm) for the folding part of the cover. Add 2 in. (5 cm) all around for seam allowances.

7 From the undyed calico and using the largest piece of dyed fabric as a guide, cut two rectangles; these form the inside of the cover. Cut one of these in half; these pieces will be the sleeves. Cut four pieces of undyed calico to slightly larger than the size of your device. These will hold the card stiffeners.

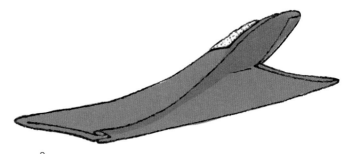

8 Take the rectangle of fabric for the tab and fold it in half lengthwise. Fold the raw ends under and press. Unfold and then stitch the hook (stiff) side of the hook-and-loop tape at the top of the rectangle to one side. Fold the raw edges under again, including the short end near the top of the tape, and topstitch around the three folded sides.

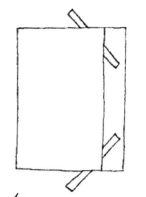 

9 Stitch the feather motif panel to the larger piece of dyed fabric as shown, using several rows of stitching for a nice effect. Stitch the loop (soft) side of the hook-and-loop tape to the opposite side of the outer cover.

10 Press and stitch a double ¾-in. (2-cm) hem on one long side of each of the sleeve pieces. On one of the sleeves insert two of the pieces of elastic where shown.

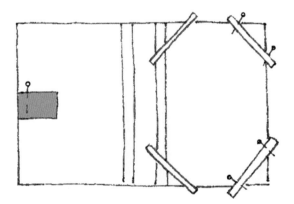

11 Place the hemmed sleeve pieces on the larger undyed piece of calico, which will form the inner cover. Line up the outer edges and pin the remaining two pieces of elastic in-place. Place the tab on the left-hand side, with the hook-and-loop tape facing down and the raw edges aligned, and pin in place.

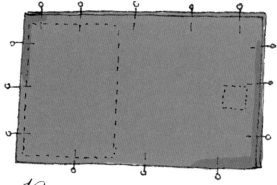

12 Place the dyed and stenciled outer cover face down over the inner cover, with the motif on the left, and pin in place.

13 Stitch all around through both layers, taking a ¾-in. (2-cm) seam allowance and leaving a small gap halfway along one of the long sides through which the cover can be turned right side out.

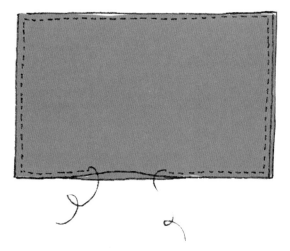

14 Turn through to the right side, press, and topstitch around all the edges—this will also close the opening.

15 Place the remaining undyed pieces of calico together in pairs before stitching round three sides of each using a straight stitch. Turn them right side out and insert the pieces of card. Tuck the fabric on the remaining open side in and topstitch closed before inserting the stiffeners into the calico sleeves.

appliquéd
hand Towel

Revamp some plain white towels with an indigo dyed panel. In this case, we have used a leaf stencil to batik and a light indigo vat. Blue and white has always been a good color combination!

You will need

- Fern template (see page 141)
- Tracing or greaseproof paper
- Pencil
- Shiny card
- Sharp scissors or craft knife
- Plain white towel
- Piece of linen, 6 in. (15 cm) long and 3 in. (8 cm) wider than your towel
- 2 oz (50 g) soya wax flakes
- Double boiler or microwave
- Old newspapers
- Sponge applicator
- Prepared indigo vat (see page 8)
- Rubber gloves and apron
- Bowls for soaking and rinsing
- White household vinegar
- Washing detergent
- Iron
- Paper towels
- Basic sewing kit

1 Trace the fern template on page 141 onto shiny card and cut out your stencil (see pages 55–56).

2 Measure the width of your towel, adding 1 in. (2 cm) to the width. Cut your linen to that width by the depth you require, plus 1 in. (2 cm).

3 Melt the wax in a double boiler on the hob or place it in a glass container and heat in a microwave in 30-second bursts—it is important not to overheat the wax. Work out how best to place the stencil on the fabric—depending on the width of your towel, you may want to repeat the stencil three or more times. Protecting your work surface with old newspapers, use a sponge applicator to apply the melted wax through the stencil (see page 56). Repeat as desired. Leave the wax to set.

4 Soak the fabric in clean, tepid water for a couple of hours and squeeze out any excess water. Dye and rinse, following the instructions on pages 13–14. Remove excess wax by scraping it off with the blade of a knife, then wash in detergent and dry. Remove any remaining wax by laying paper towels over the fabric and pressing gently with a cool iron.

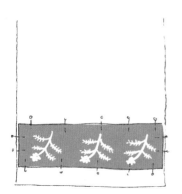

5 Once all the wax is removed, press all the four sides under by ½ in. (1 cm) to the wrong side so that the fabric panel is the same width as your towel. Trim away any excess fabric.

6 Pin the stenciled linen panel to the towel and topstitch in place.

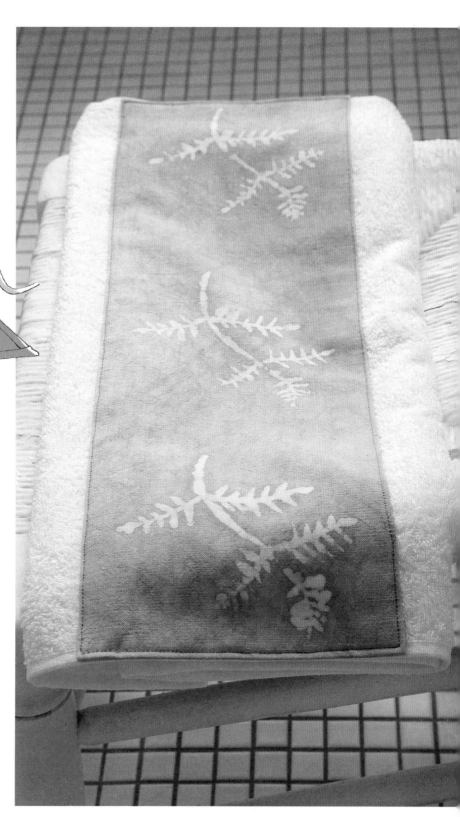

Child's *Teepee*

Sit inside this teepee and the light shines through the star shapes that were batik waxed onto it before the calico was dyed a deep, deep indigo blue! This is a really fun way to make a play tent for the garden.

You will need

- 2¼ yds (2 m) unbleached calico, 54 in. (140 cm) wide
- Basic sewing kit
- Sewing machine
- Star templates (see page 139)
- Tracing or greaseproof paper
- Pencil
- Shiny card
- Sharp scissors or craft knife
- 7 oz (200 g) soya wax flakes
- Double boiler or microwave
- Old newspapers
- Sponge applicator
- Prepared indigo vat (see page 8)
- Bowls for soaking and rinsing
- Rubber gloves and apron
- White household vinegar
- Washing detergent
- Iron
- Paper towels
- Approx. 19 yds (17 m) red bias binding
- Six 72-in. (183-cm) garden canes

1 Lay your fabric out flat and, starting at the left-hand side, mark along the top edge at the following intervals: 1 in. (2.5 cm), 21¾ in. (55 cm), 2 in. (5 cm), 21¾ in. (55 cm), 2 in. (5 cm), 21¾ in. (55 cm), 1 in. (2.5 cm). Now mark along the bottom edge, again starting at the left-hand side as follows: 11 in. (27.5 cm), 2 in. (5 cm), 21¾ in. (55 cm), 2 in. (5 cm), 21¾ in. (55 cm), 11 in. (27.5 cm).

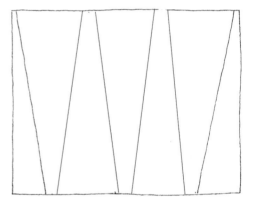

Draw diagonal lines as shown and cut out along these lines. Neaten the raw edges of each piece, either by overlocking or by using a close zigzag stitch on your sewing machine.

2 Trace the star templates on page 139 onto shiny card and cut out your stencils (see pages 55–56).

3 Melt the wax in a double boiler on the hob or place it in a glass container and heat in a microwave in 30-second bursts (see page 56). Protect your work surface with old newspapers. Place the star stencils over each cut-out panel in turn and use a sponge applicator to apply the melted wax through the cut-out stencils (see page 56), positioning the stars randomly.

4 Soak the fabric in clean, tepid water for a couple of hours and squeeze out any excess water. Dye and rinse, following the instructions on pages 13–14. Remove the excess wax by scraping it off with the blade of a knife, then wash in detergent and dry. Remove any remaining wax by laying paper towels over the fabric and pressing gently with a cool iron.

5 With right sides together, stitch all the full-size "triangles" together with the narrowest parts at the top. Cut 1 yd (1 m) of the bias binding and fold it in half lengthwise. Stitch along the length, close to the fold. Cut two 4-in. (10-cm) lengths to make the loops, and cut the rest into two equal pieces to make the ties for step 6. Pin the smaller triangles to the outside edges of the main piece, inserting the loops halfway down the seams; these will be inside the door flaps. Press the seams open.

6 Bind the bottom of the teepee with bias binding (see page 135). Repeat with both side hems, which will form the opening, inserting the bias binding ties halfway up so that they are level with the loops on the inside.

7 Pin bias binding along the top of the tee pee fabric, folding it in half lengthwise and leaving a length of 12 in. (30 cm) either side to form the ties. Machine stitch in place.

8 Cover all the remaining seams with bias binding: fold under at the top and bottom and stitch down either side of the bias binding to create channels into which the canes can be inserted. Tie the canes together loosely at the top.

tab-topped *curtains*

Tab-topped curtains with a simple motif repeated along the hem are a charming way to decorate a window. Flower shapes work well with batik.

You will need

- Two lengths of unbleached calico (see Calculating fabric, below)
- Flower template (see page 141)
- Tracing or greaseproof paper
- Pencil
- Shiny card
- Sharp scissors or craft knife
- 4 oz (100 g) soya wax flakes per yard (metre) width of fabric
- Double boiler or microwave
- Old newspapers
- Sponge applicator
- Cotton webbing tape, 1 in. (2.5 cm) wide and the length of your curtain width, plus 6 in. (15 cm)
- Prepared indigo vat (see page 8)
- Rubber gloves and apron
- Bowls for soaking and rinsing
- White household vinegar
- Washing detergent
- Iron and paper towels
- Basic sewing kit

1 Trace the flower template on page 141 onto shiny card and cut out your stencil (see pages 55–56).

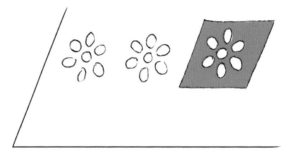

2 Melt the wax in a double boiler on the hob or place it in a glass container and heat in a microwave in 30-second bursts (see page 56). Protect your work surface with old newspapers. Place the flower stencil over the bottom edge of each curtain, approximately 8 in. (20 cm) from the raw edge, and use a sponge applicator to apply the melted wax through the cut-out stencil (see page 56). Leave the wax to dry.

3 Soak the fabric in clean, tepid water for a couple of hours, and then squeeze out the excess water. Dye both the fabric and the webbing, following the instructions on pages 13–14. Rinse well, adding vinegar to the final rinse. Remove the excess wax by scraping it off with the blade of a knife, then wash in detergent and dry. Iron over some absorbent paper towels to remove the last of the wax.

Calculating Fabric

Measure the required drop of the curtain and add on 13 in. (32.5 cm) for the tabs and bottom hem. Measure the width and add on 4 in. (10 cm) for the side hems, plus an extra 50% for fullness (increase this amount if you want a more gathered curtain.) Cut two pieces of fabric to these measurements.

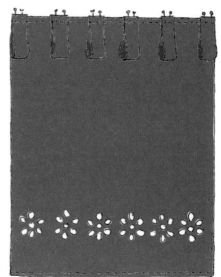

4 Trim the bottom hem edges where they may have frayed during dyeing. Remove a strip 8 in. (20 cm) deep from the top of each dyed curtain and cut each piece into six strips. Fold each tab in half lengthwise, wrong sides together, and machine stitch, taking a ⅜-in. (1-cm) seam allowance. Trim the seam allowance, then press the seam open, centering it in the middle of the tab. Turn the tab right side out.

5 Turn under and stitch a double 1-in. (2.5-cm) hem on each side of each curtain. Fold up and stitch a double 2-in. (5-cm) hem along the bottom of each curtain. Fold each tab in half, with the seam on the inside, and place along the top of the curtain, right sides together and with the raw edges level, so that the tabs are pointing downward. Pin, then machine stitch in place, taking a ¾-in. (2-cm) seam allowance.

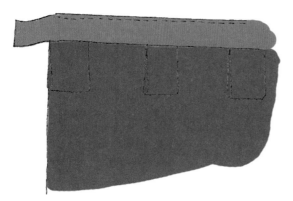

6 Pin and stitch the dyed webbing tape along the tops of the curtains, covering the ends of the stitched tabs. Leave 1½ in. (4 cm) overhanging at each end—this will be folded in to cover the raw edges.

7 Fold the tape overlap in at each end and then fold the tape over to the wrong side of the curtains. Press in place and then pin and machine stitch along the bottom edge of the tape to secure.

chapter 4
Tie-dyeing

Tying bunched fabric in order to prevent the dye from reaching parts of the fabric produces some lovely patterns. This tie-dye effect is very well known, sometimes by the name "shibori kumo", and it works particularly well with indigo.

Tie-dyeing Techniques

When tie-dyeing, the fabric can just be tied using string or elastic bands at intervals, but a more varied effect can be achieved by wrapping the fabric around stones before soaking and dyeing. The stones can be in a variety of shapes and sizes, for a more random pattern, or similar-sized for a regular pattern. The instructions below are for tie-dyeing with stones, but the technique is just the same if you are tying fabric without stones: simply bunch up your fabric, at regular intervals or in a random pattern, and tie tightly with string or elastic.

You will need

- Fabric
- Selection of stones
- String
- Prepared indigo vat (see page 8)
- Rubber gloves and apron
- Bowls for soaking and rinsing
- White household vinegar
- Washing detergent
- Scissors

1 Gather together your stones, choosing a variety of sizes and shapes depending on the effect you're after. Make sure the stones are clean.

2 Starting in the center of your piece of fabric, wrap the fabric around the first stone and tie very tightly with string.

3 Repeat until you have enough stones tied in place, working outward from the center.

4 Soak the fabric in clean, cold water for a few hours. Remove from the bowl and gently squeeze out all the excess water.

5 Dye the fabric in your prepared indigo vat, following the instructions on pages 13–14. Repeat the dipping process until you have reached the desired shade. Rinse the fabric, adding vinegar to the final rinse, then let it dry.

6 Using scissors, carefully snip the strings holding the stones in place. The undyed fabric will be revealed, forming a ring pattern. These are the areas the dye could not reach. Wash the fabric and dry it.

striped
linen curtain

Large pieces of fabric can be tricky to dye in a pan at home, but pleating the fabric and tying it tightly will enable you to dye large, curtain-sized pieces quite easily. Ready-made curtains can also be dyed in this way!

You will need

- Ready-made linen curtain or length of linen, pre-washed and dried (see Calculating fabric, below)
- Elastic or string for the ties
- Prepared indigo vat (see page 8)
- Rubber gloves and apron
- Bowls for soaking and rinsing
- White household vinegar
- Washing detergent

1 Pleat the fabric along its length, keeping the pleats as straight and even as possible.

2 Tie all along this pleated length of fabric, making sure that the ties are tied really tight and are evenly spaced.

3 Soak the fabric in clean, cold water for a few hours, then squeeze out the excess water. Dye, following the instructions on pages 13–14. Very large pieces of fabric may need to be formed into a coil shape in order to fit into the dyeing vat. Wear rubber gloves and work the fibers under the surface in order to achieve a good color.

Calculating Fabric

Measure the required drop of the curtain and add on 5 in. (12.5 cm) for the hems at the top and bottom. (This is for a standard taped heading.) For the width, each curtain needs to be 1.5–2 times the width of the curtain track before being gathered.

4 Rinse in clean water, adding vinegar to the final rinse. Remove the ties and then wash with detergent in the usual way and allow to dry. Press the fabric and either hang the curtain or follow the instructions in Step 5 to make up.

5 Press 1 in. (2.5 cm) to the wrong side on either side of the fabric, pin, and then machine stitch in place. Press 1 in. (2.5 cm) to the wrong side along the top edge and pin in place. Cut the heading tape to the desired width, adding 1 in. (2.5 cm). Pin along the top of the curtain, folding ½ in. (1 cm) under at each end, and then machine stitch in place. Finally, fold a double 2-in. (5-cm) hem at the bottom of the curtain and either machine or hand stitch in place. Gather the curtain to the desired width and hang.

tie-dyed  T-shirt

An old white or light-colored T-shirt can be given a new lease on life if you tie-dye it! Folding and tying it tightly will give you a random striped effect.

1 Fold the T-shirt into loose pleats. Horizontal folds will produce horizontal stripes.

You will need

- Plain, light-colored T-shirt, pre-washed and dried
- Elastic or string for ties
- Prepared indigo vat (see page 8)
- Rubber gloves and apron
- Bowls for soaking and rinsing
- Scissors
- White household vinegar
- Washing detergent

2 Tie very tightly at intervals across the length of the folded T-shirt. The more ties you use, the paler your T-shirt will be; using fewer ties produces darker results.

3 Soak the tied T-shirt in clean water to prepare it for dyeing. Dye following the instructions on pages 13–14, repeating the dipping until the desired shade is reached.

4 Rinse in plenty of clean water, adding vinegar to the final rinse. Carefully remove the ties with scissors and then wash the T-shirt with washing detergent. Allow to dry.

reversible *Tablecloth*

A tie-dyed tablecloth finished with a patterned bias binding edging—just turn it over for a plain tablecloth!

You will need

- Fabric large enough for a tablecloth (see Calculating fabric, below), pre-washed and dried—a large cotton sheet is ideal
- Fabric marker pen
- Basic sewing kit
- Elastic or string for tying
- Prepared indigo vat (see page 8)
- Rubber gloves and apron
- Bowls for soaking and rinsing
- White household vinegar
- Washing detergent
- Patterned bias binding 1 in. (2.5 cm) wide
- Sewing machine
- Iron

1 Fold your fabric into four and measure along the top of this square of fabric. Use this measurement to draw a curved line from corner to corner from the center of the fabric.

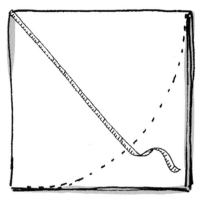

2 Keeping the fabric folded, cut through the four layers one at a time, carefully following the marked line. This will give you a perfect circle.

Calculating Fabric

Decide how long you want the drop on your tablecloth to be. This could be anything from 8–12 in. (20–30 cm). Measure the diameter of your table and add twice the desired drop to this measurement—this will be the diameter of your cloth. Cut a square of fabric to this size, adding on ½ in. (1 cm) for seam allowances.

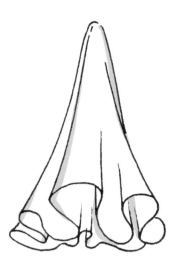

3 Take hold of the center point of the tablecloth and shake the folds out so that the fabric drapes gracefully.

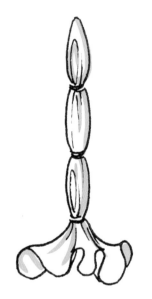

4 Working from the center out toward the edge of the cloth, place ties at irregular intervals along the bundled cloth. This will result in a sunburst pattern. Ensure that the ties are really tight.

5 Soak the tablecloth in clean, cold water for a couple of hours, then squeeze out the excess water. Dye the fabric, following the instructions on pages 13–14. As this is a large piece, you'll need to work the fibers under the surface for a few seconds.

6 Rinse in several changes of clean water, adding vinegar to the final rinse. Remove the ties, wash with detergent. and allow to dry.

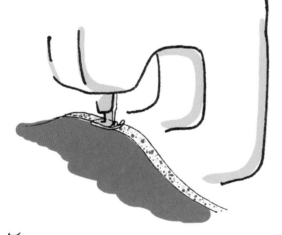

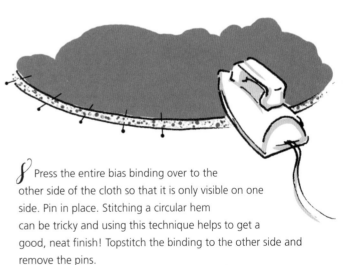

7 When the tablecloth is dry, press with an iron and then pin one raw edge of the bias binding around the edge of the entire cloth. Machine stitch in place, stitching ¼ in. (6 mm) from the edge and removing the pins as you go.

8 Press the entire bias binding over to the other side of the cloth so that it is only visible on one side. Pin in place. Stitching a circular hem can be tricky and using this technique helps to get a good, neat finish! Topstitch the binding to the other side and remove the pins.

wall *hanging*

Tying the fabric from the center outward produces a dramatic "sunburst" pattern. Hang the dyed and stitched fabric on a rod to make it into an attractive wall hanging.

You will need

- Plain fabric, pre-washed and dried
- String or elastic for ties
- Prepared indigo vat (see page 8)
- Rubber gloves and apron
- Bowls for soaking and rinsing
- White household vinegar
- Washing detergent
- Basic sewing kit
- Sewing machine
- Pole or rod, for hanging

1 Decide what size you want your wall hanging to be and cut the fabric to this size, remembering to add 2 in. (5 cm) to the width and 2–3 in. (5–7.5 cm) to the length for the hems and rod casing. (The depth of the casing will depend on the size of the hanging rod.) Find the approximate center of the fabric by holding it in one hand and shaking it, allowing it to drape and fall into irregular pleats.

2 Starting at the center, tie tight ties along the length of the bunched fabric.

3 Soak in clean water for a few hours and then dip into the prepared indigo vat until the desired shade is achieved.

4 Rinse in plenty of clean, cold water until all the excess dye is removed, adding vinegar to the final rinse. Remove the ties, wash the dyed fabric with washing detergent, and allow to dry.

5 Leaving the top edge for now, press and then machine stitch a double ½-in. (1-cm) hem along the sides and bottom.

6 Making sure that it is large enough to allow your pole or rod to be inserted, machine stitch a deeper double hem along the top edge of the fabric. Insert the pole or rod and then hang.

Table runner

Using stones tied tightly into linen produces some gorgeous patterns. A table runner is a quick and simple way to dress a table stylishly.

You will need

- Undyed linen fabric, approx. 15 in. (38 cm) wide by the length of your table plus 4 in. (10 cm)
- Selection of stones
- String for tying
- Prepared indigo vat (see page 8)
- Bowls for soaking and rinsing
- Rubber gloves and apron
- White household vinegar
- Washing detergent
- Iron
- Basic sewing kit

1 Select stones in a variety of sizes and shapes in order to give you an interesting and varied effect.

2 Take your piece of linen and, starting in the center, bunch the linen around one of the stones and tie very tightly with string.

3 Repeat with more stones, spacing them as evenly as you can until you have enough stones tied in place.

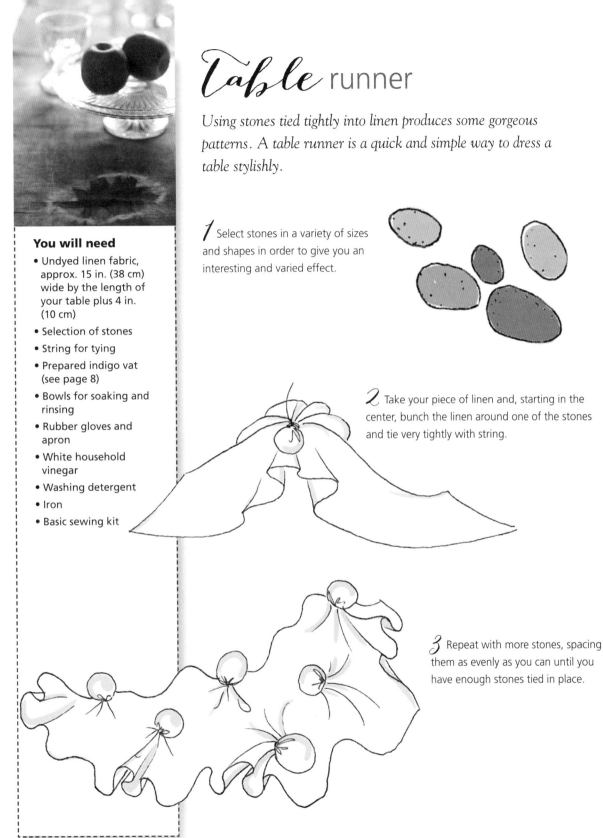

4 Soak the linen in clean, cold water for a few hours.

5 Remove the linen from the water, squeeze gently to remove some of the excess water, and dye following the instructions on pages 13–14. Repeat the dipping process until you have reached the desired shade.

6 Rinse in several changes of clean water, adding vinegar to the final rinse. Using scissors, snip the strings holding the stones in place. The undyed fabric around the stones will be revealed in a pretty ring pattern. Wash in detergent and allow to dry, then iron on the correct setting.

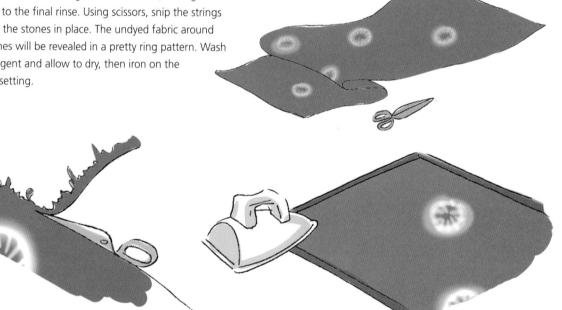

7 Once dried and pressed, trim away any frayed edges using scissors and cut to size.

8 Press and turn over a double 1-in. (2.5-cm) hem on all four sides before machine stitching in place.

chapter 5

Tie-dyeing with wood

This technique, also known as "shibori itajime," uses pieces of wood or heavy cardstock (card) to clamp pleated fabric tightly before dyeing in order to prevent the dye from reaching all of the fabric. Because the fabric is folded many times to fit the size of the wood, this is a great way to dye quite large pieces of fabric easily.

wood tie-dye Techniques

This technique produces a light and open pattern with attractive repeats—particularly if the fabric is pleated vertically along its length. You can also vary the effect by pleating again across these pleats horizontally or diagonally. The pleated fabric is then placed between two pieces of wood and the whole thing is tied together tightly with string. As the items are only dipped into the indigo dye vat for a few moments, heavy card stock can also be used to hold the fabric in place. After dipping and airing, the items must remain clamped until after the final rinse in order to prevent any dye from seeping into the undyed parts within the clamps.

You will need

- Two pieces of wood or heavy cardstock (card)
- String
- Prepared indigo vat (see page 8)
- Rubber gloves and apron
- Bowls for soaking and rinsing
- White household vinegar
- Washing detergent

1 Fold the fabric into vertical pleats, then pleat again across the width. This will produce a checked pattern. The folded piece should be slightly wider than your pieces of wood or cardstock (card)—the amount of fabric exposed at the sides, top, and bottom will dictate how broad or narrow your stripes will be.

2 Place the pleated fabric between the two pieces of wood.

3 Tie string tightly around the wood-and-fabric sandwich.

4 Soak in cold, clean water for a few hours. The wood will float, so weigh it down with something like a brick.

5 Squeeze as much water out of the fabric as possible. Dip into the indigo vat by sliding the prepared fabric down the side of the pan; remember, you are aiming to disturb the surface as little as possible (see pages 13–14). Remove after a few moments, letting the excess dye dribble back into the vat with as little splashing as possible.

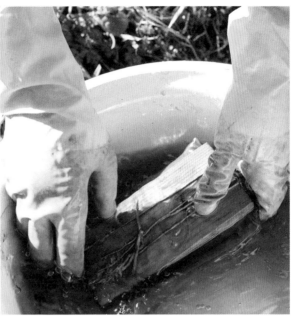

_6_ Allow the dyed fabric to air—still clamped between the wood—opening the edges of the pleats to allow oxygen to develop the dye. Repeat the dipping process if you want a deeper shade of blue, airing and allowing the dye to develop each time.

_7_ With the fabric still clamped and tied, rinse well in several changes of cold, clean water, adding vinegar to the final rinse (see pages 13–14).

_8_ Cut the tied string and remove the wood.

_9_ Unfold the pleated fabric, wash in detergent and allow to dry.

garden *canopy*

A freestanding awning for the garden, propped up on bamboo canes, makes the perfect place to rest, recline, and read while shaded from the sun!

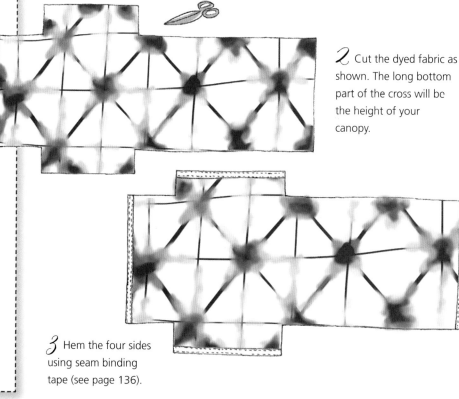

You will need

- 1¾ x 4¼ yds (1.5 x 3.8 m) linen fabric
- Two pieces of wood, approx. 8½ x 11 x ¾ in. (22 x 28 x 2 cm)
- String
- Prepared indigo vat (see page 8)
- Rubber gloves and apron
- Bowls for soaking and rinsing
- White household vinegar
- Washing detergent
- 20 in. (50 cm) webbing tape cut into four equal pieces
- Basic sewing kit
- Reel of seam binding tape
- Four garden canes, cut down to preferred height
- Mallet
- Eight tent pegs
- 22 yds (20 m) thin rope or piping cord

1 Fold the fabric vertically into pleats a little wider than the wood, then fold the bottom right corner over to the left-hand edge to form a triangle. Keep folding the fabric over in triangles until you reach the end. This will create the diagonal lines. Clamp between the pieces of wood, then soak and dye, along with the webbing tape, following the instructions on pages 99–101. Rinse, wash, allow to dry, then press.

2 Cut the dyed fabric as shown. The long bottom part of the cross will be the height of your canopy.

3 Hem the four sides using seam binding tape (see page 136).

4 Fold each piece of dyed webbing tape in half and insert into the corner seams, as shown. The raw edges should be lined up and the folded edge facing away from the seam. Pin in place.

5 With right sides together, stitch down each of the four corner seams, taking a ¾-in. (2-cm) seam allowance.

6 Press the stitched seams over to one side, in each case folding away from the short side.

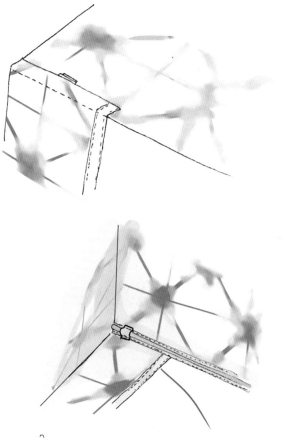

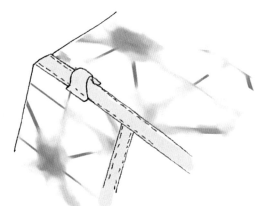

7 Cut four strips of seam binding, each 2½ in. (6 cm) long. Cover the raw edges of the canop with seam binding and stitch in place. Then position the 2½-in. (6-cm) strips of seam binding over the seam binding near the top of the canopy to form "loops," tucking the raw edges in on each side. These loops will hold the garden canes in position once the canopy is erected.

8 Turn the canopy right side out and place the four canes in the loops of seam binding, one at each corner.

9 Using a mallet, bash the tent pegs firmly into the ground. Tie the ropes through the webbing loops and then loosely onto the pegs. Pull the ropes firmly and adjust pegs, canes, and ropes as needed before knotting the ropes tightly.

linen *skirt*

This simple wraparound skirt is both easy to make and easy to wear, and the perfect choice for hot summer days! The tie-dyed pattern is regular and pleasing.

You will need

- Length of undyed fabric (see Calculating fabric, below)
- Two pieces of wood, approximately 4 x 6 x ¾ in. (10 x 15 x 2 cm)
- String
- Prepared indigo vat (see page 8)
- Rubber gloves and apron
- Bowls for soaking and rinsing
- White household vinegar
- Washing detergent
- Basic sewing kit
- Sewing machine

1 Fold the fabric vertically into pleats a little wider than the wood, then pleat it horizontally. Clamp, soak, and dye the fabric, following the instructions on pages 99–101. Rinse, wash, allow to dry, and press. Trim away any frayed edges.

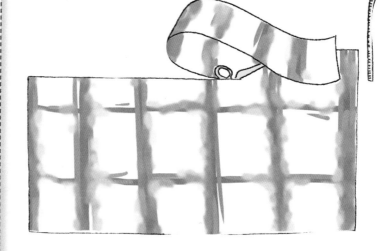

2 Measure and cut a strip of fabric 6 in. (15 cm) deep from one of the long edges.

Calculating Fabric

Decide how long you want the skirt to be and measure from your waist to this point.

Add on 3 in. (8 cm) for the top and bottom hems and another 6 in. (15 cm) for the waist ties. Measure one and a half times around your waist and add on 3 in. (8 cm) for the side hems. Cut the fabric to these measurements.

3 Fold this strip of fabric in half lengthwise and then fold both raw edges under and stitch close to the fold. Cut this in half to create two ties.

4 Turn a double ¾-in. (2-cm) hem along both side edges and along the bottom hem of the skirt. Using the zigzag setting on your sewing machine, stitch along the top of the skirt.

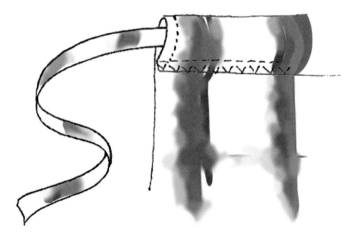

5 Turn the zigzag edge over to the wrong side of the skirt, creating a hem of 2 in. (5 cm) and insert the end of one tie into each end of the waist channel, as shown. Straight stitch with the sewing machine down each short side of the channel, trapping the ties in place, and along the long edge, just above the zigzag stitching.

6 To wear, wrap the skirt around the waist and tie at the side.

silk *scarf*

Silk scarf blanks are available from craft and dye shops. Clamping the silk between pieces of wood after pleating produces a subtle effect with a regular pattern.

You will need

- Silk scarf, pre-washed and dried
- Two pieces of wood, approximately 6 x 3 x ¾ in. (15 x 8 x 2 cm)
- String
- Scissors
- Prepared indigo vat (see page 8)
- Rubber gloves and apron
- Bowls for soaking and rinsing
- White household vinegar
- Washing detergent

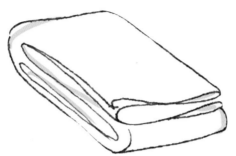

1 Fold the scarf vertically into pleats a little wider than the wood and then pleat horizontally.

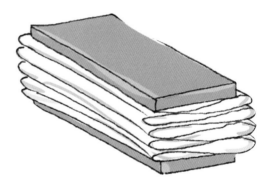

2 Place the pleated scarf between the two pieces of wood.

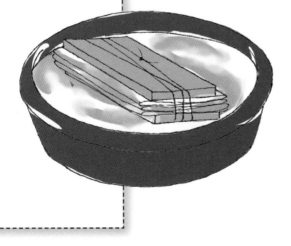

3 Tie the two pieces of wood together with string. Tie tightly and knot the ends securely so that the scarf is clamped inside. Soak in a bowl or bucket of clean, cold water—you may need to weigh the wood down with a brick as the wood will float!

4 Remove from the water and squeeze to remove some of the excess water. Place in your prepared indigo vat to dye the fabric. Dip several times, allowing the dye to develop each time, until the desired shade is achieved.

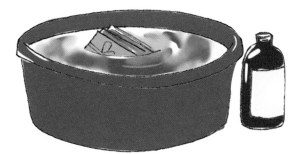

5 Rinse several times in clean, cold water, remembering to add vinegar to the final rinse.

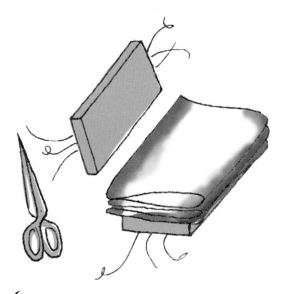

6 Cut the string and remove the two pieces of wood to reveal the areas of undyed fabric. Shake out the scarf, wash in detergent, and hang on the line to dry.

swedish
roll-up shade

A simple roll-up covering looks great at any window. The regular open pattern produced when dyeing fabric pleated and clamped between wood works well with this style of shade.

1 Fold the fabric vertically into pleats a little wider than the wood, then pleat it horizontally. Clamp, soak, and dye the fabric, following the instructions on pages 99–101. Allow to dry, press, and trim away any frayed edges.

You will need

- Length of undyed fabric (see Calculating fabric, below)
- Two pieces of wood approximately 6 x 3 x ¾ in. (15 x 8 x 2 cm) [
- String
- Prepared indigo vat (see page 8)
- Rubber gloves and apron
- Bowls for soaking and rinsing
- White household vinegar
- Washing detergent
- Basic sewing kit
- Sewing machine
- Two D-rings
- Hook-and-loop tape, 1 in. (2.5 cm) shorter than the width of your blind
- Wooden lathe, 1 in. (2.5 cm) shorter than the width of your shade
- 1 x 1 in. (2.5 x 2.5 cm) wooden batten, 1 in. (2.5 cm) shorter than the width of your blind
- Staple gun
- 2 brass screw eyes
- Thin cord or twine
- Cleat for the cord

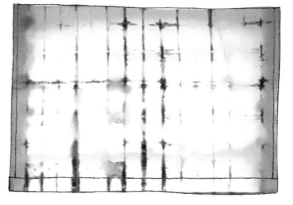

2 Turn a double 1-in. (2.5-cm) hem to the wrong side on both sides of the fabric and stitch these side seams in place. Turn a double 2-in. (5-cm) to the wrong side along the bottom edge and stitch close to the fold to create a channel for the wooden lathe.

Calculating Fabric

Decide how long and wide you want the finished shade to be; it's up to you whether you hang the shade on the inside or the outside of the window recess. Add 4 in. (10 cm) to the width to allow for the side hems and 10 in. (25 cm) to the length to allow for the top and bottom hems, plus the fabric needed for the tabs (see step 3, overleaf).

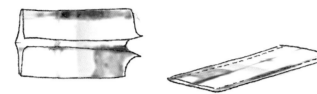 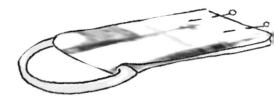

3 Cut a 6-in. (15-cm) strip off the top of your dyed fabric and use it to cut two rectangles, each 6 x 4 in. (15 x 10 cm). Fold each rectangle in half lengthwise and then turn both raw edges under and machine stitch along the open long edge to create two tabs.

4 Place each tab through a D-ring and pin so the raw edges line up with each other.

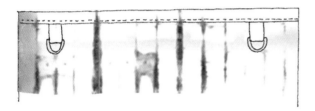 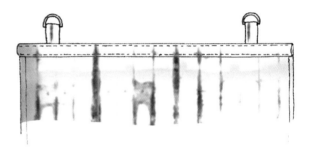

5 Pin the D-ring tabs in place along the top of the fabric, right sides together and with raw edges level and approximately 10 in. (25 cm) in from each outside edge. Take the loop side of the hook-and-loop tape and pin it along the top of the shade, over the D-ring tabs. Stitch the lower edge (nearest to the tabs) only.

6 Fold the hook-and-loop tape over to the wrong side of the shade and stitch along the bottom edge of the tape, ensuring that the D-ring tabs are clear of the stitch line.

7 Insert the wooden lathe into the pocket at the bottom of the shade.

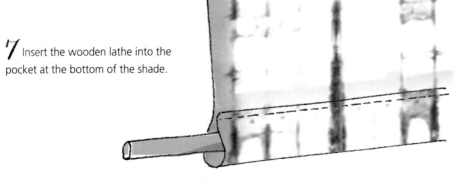

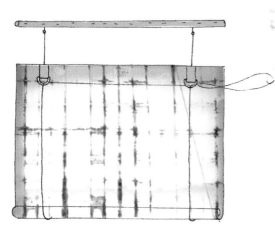

8 Attach the hook side of the hook-and-loop tape to the wooden batten with a staple gun. Fix the screw eyes into the underside of the wooden batten, so that they are in line with the D-ring tabs on the shade. Tie the cord ends to these screw eyes and bring them down behind the shade and up the front, threading them through the D-rings and down to the side where the cleat is positioned.

9 Pull the cords so that the shade rolls up to the top. Knot the cord ends together, trimming away any excess cord a little below the knot. Fix the cleat to the wall or window frame as desired.

quilted *placemats*

Quilting is easier than most people think, and pinning and stitching with care will give a neat finish. A contrast patterned binding sets off the blue and white dyed fabric perfectly!

1 Fold the fabric vertically into pleats a little wider than the wood, then pleat it horizontally. Clamp, soak, and dye the fabric, following the instructions on pages 99–101. Rinse, adding vinegar to the final rinse. Wash in detergent, dry, and press.

You will need

- 28 x 10 in. (70 x 25 cm) white cotton fabric per mat
- Two pieces of wood approximately 10 x 3 x ¾ in. (25 x 7.5 x 2 cm)
- String
- Prepared indigo vat (see page 8)
- Rubber gloves and apron
- Bowls for soaking and rinsing
- White household vinegar
- Washing detergent
- Basic sewing kit
- Sewing machine
- 14 x 10 in. (35 x 25 cm) batting (wadding) per mat
- Small plate or saucer
- Pencil
- 1¾ yds (1½ m) floral bias binding, 1 in. (2.5 cm) wide

2 Cut the fabric in half to give two 14 x 10-in. (35 x 25-cm) rectangles. Place one piece on your work surface, with the batting (wadding) on top, then place the remaining piece on top of the batting. Pin all three layers together.

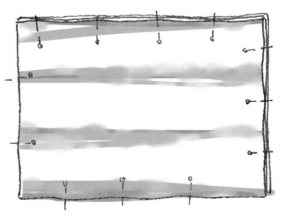

3 Using a straight stitch on your sewing machine, quilt vertical lines through all three layers, starting from the center and working outward.

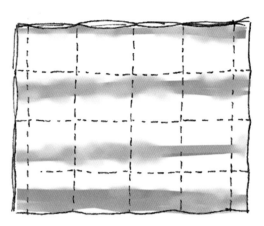

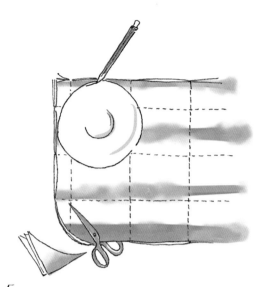

4 Repeat to quilt the horizontal lines across the mat, again starting from center and working out toward the outside edges. This will prevent the layers from moving about too muc and also adds visual interesth.

5 Use a small plate or saucer to draw a curved edge at each of the four corners. Trim away the excess fabric, including any layers that may have moved during quilting.

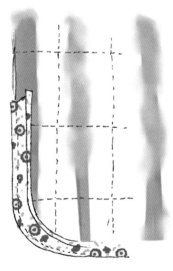

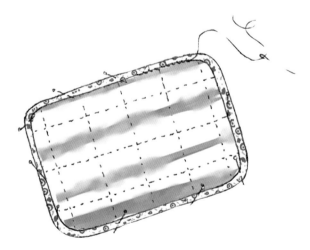

6 Stitch one edge of the bias binding all around the upper edge of the front of the placemat, starting and finishing at the center of one of the long sides. Finish by neatly folding one end of the bias binding under and tucking the other end inside before stitching over the join.

7 Fold the bias binding over to the back of the mat, pin, and neatly stitch it in place.

chapter 6

Tie-dyeing with Tubes

A dramatic effect can be achieved on narrower pieces of fabric by using a piece of plastic tubing. This is also known as "shibori arashi." Fabric is wrapped loosely around the tube and tied in place with string; the fabric is then pushed down to one end. The dye can only get to the areas of fabric on the outside of the folds, which creates a crisp, attractive pattern.

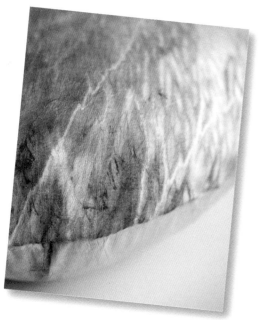

Tube Tie-dyeing Techniques

Depending on how many times you wrap the fabric around the tube, and how tight the folds are, you can create a variety of patterns using this method. The fabric nearest the tube will have the faintest pattern, while the fabric on the outside of the tube will be a darker blue. The fabric within the folds will remain undyed.

You will need

- Fabric
- 18 in. (45 cm) plastic tube, 3in. (8 cm) in diameter
- String
- Prepared indigo vat (see page 8)
- Rubber gloves and apron
- Bowls for soaking and rinsing
- White household vinegar
- Washing detergent

1 Wrap your fabric widthways around the tube and loosely tie with string in a crisscross pattern up and down the tube.

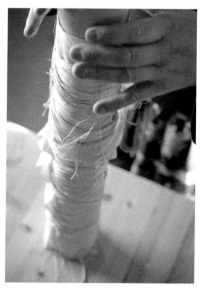

2 Push the fabric and string all the way down to one end of the tube, as far as it will go.

3 Soak in cold, clean water for a couple of hours, and squeeze out any excess water.

4 Dye in your prepared indigo vat, following the instructions for plain dyeing on pages 13–14.

5 Rinse several times in clean, cold water, adding vinegar to the final rinse. Carefully cut through the string, unwrap the fabric, wash in detergent, and allow to dry.

round pillow *cover*

Silk takes indigo dye on beautifully and, as it's quite a fine fabric, it also works well with this "arashi" style of tie-dyeing. The more the fabric is scrunched down the tubes it's wrapped around, the better!

1 Tie and dye the silk fabric, following the instructions on pages 122–123. When dry, carefully iron the silk on the correct setting.

2 Fold the newspaper into four. Using a ruler, mark the paper at several intervals 9 in. (23 cm) from the center. Cut along these marked points and open the newspaper out to create a large circle.

3 Pin the pattern onto one of the pieces of silk and cut out.

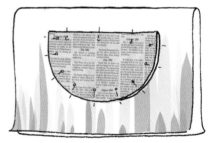

4 Fold the second piece of silk in half. Fold the paper pattern in half and place it on the folded silk, 4 in. (10 cm) away from the folded edge of the fabric. Pin in place

You will need

- Two pieces of silk, each measuring at least 25 x 25 in. (62.5 x 62.5 cm)
- 18 in. (45 cm) plastic tube, 3 in. (8 cm) in diameter
- String
- Prepared indigo vat (see page 8)
- Rubber gloves and apron
- Bowls for soaking and rinsing
- White household vinegar
- Washing detergent
- Large sheet of newspaper
- Pencil and ruler
- Scissors
- Sewing machine
- Basic sewing kit
- 18-in. (45-cm) pillow form (cushion pad)

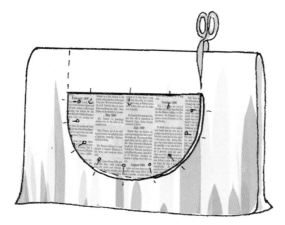

5 Starting from the folded edge of the fabric, cut out the elongated semicircle shape.

6 Now cut along the folded edge to create two elongated semicircles and sew a double 1-in. (2.5-cm) hem along both straight edges.

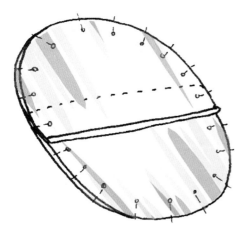

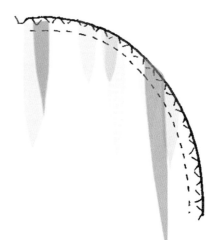

7 Place the hemmed pieces on top of the circle of fabric, right sides together, and with the hemmed edges overlapping. Pin in place.

8 Machine stitch around the circle, taking a ¾-in. (2-cm) seam allowance. Trim any excess fabric and finish the seams with a zigzag stitch. Turn the cover right side out and insert the pillow form (cushion pad).

5 Turn the bag right side out through the opened zipper. Make a zipper pull: take a strip of fabric and fold both raw edges in toward the center. Fold in half lengthways to conceal the raw edges and topstitch to secure. Knot through the zipper head as shown.

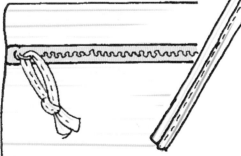

closet *liner*

Usually fabric used behind the glass in closet doors is gathered up, but here the fabric is used flat to show off the beautiful patterns achieved using this simple technique. A fresh indigo vat will give a dark indigo blue to show a crisp pattern!

1 Dye the fabric, following the instructions on pages 122–123. When dry, iron on the correct setting.

You will need

- Fine cotton fabric
- 18 in. (45 cm) plastic tube, 3in. (8 cm) in diameter
- String
- Prepared indigo vat (see page 8)
- Rubber gloves and apron
- Bowls for soaking and rinsing
- White household vinegar
- Washing detergent
- Basic sewing kit
- Four pieces of net wire, cut to just wider than your closet liners
- Eight screw eyes

2 Measure the windows of your closet or cupboard and add 4 in. (10 cm) to both the width and the drop. This is to allow for the wire or rod pockets and side hems. Cut two pieces of dyed fabric to these measurements.

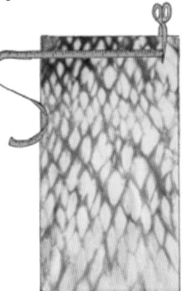

3 Turn a double 1-in. (2.5-cm) hem to the wrong side on both sides of the fabric, press, and machine stitch in place.

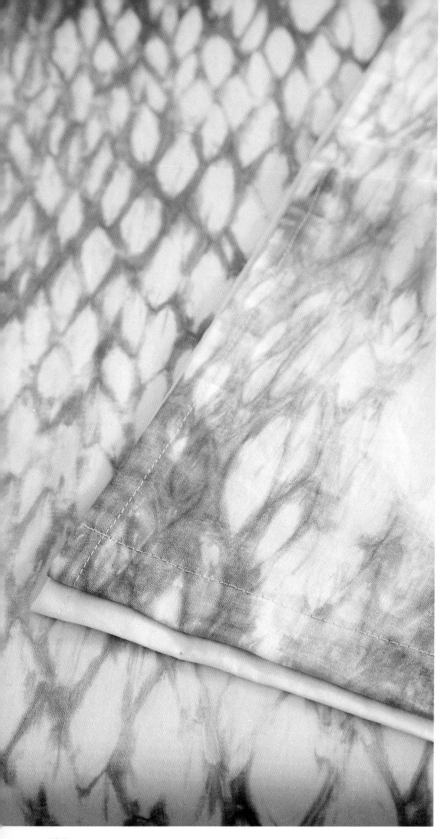

4 Turn a double 1-in. (2.5-cm) hem to the wrong side at both the top and bottom of the fabric to form two channels. Pin and then stitch in place, close to the fold. Thread the net wires or rods through the channels at the top and bottom.

5 Fix screw eyes to the inside of the doors to attach the closet liners to, which should lie flat as opposed to gathered to allow you to see the beautiful patterns produced by this dyeing technique.

Sewing Techniques

Most of the techniques you will need are described in the project instructions, but there are a few extra bits of information here that will help you get a good finish on your sewing.

Bias binding

Using bias binding to finish hems gives a neat, smooth finish. Bias binding is cut diagonally across the grain of the fabric, which means that it will stretch slightly. There are two ways of doing this, depending on whether the bias binding is to show on only one, or both, sides of the fabric.

For binding to show on one side only:

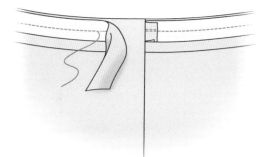

1 Open out one side of the binding and pin it around the edge of the fabric, with the right side of the binding facing the wrong side of the fabric. Stitch together along the crease line, then trim close to the seam.

2 Trim the seam and turn all the binding over to the right side of the fabric.

3 Pin the folded edge of the binding to the right side of the fabric, and topstitch in place.

For binding to show on both sides:

1 Fold the binding in half lengthwise, and fit it over the edge of the fabric. Pin in place

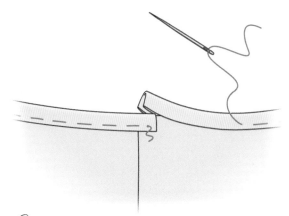

2 Stitch through the binding and the fabric, either by hand or with a machine.

3 Where the binding overlaps, trim away the binding underneath to about ½ in. (12 mm), fold under the end of the other piece of binding by about ½ in. (12 mm), and lay it over, before stitching through all layers.

Seam binding tape

Use seam binding tape to create neat straight edges, without bulky hems. The technique is the same for applying heading tape to curtains.

1 Fold the fabric over once by about ½ in. (1 cm) and press with an iron.

2 Cover the raw edge of the fabric with the seam binding tape and pin in place, just below the fold line, before topstitching along each side of the tape.

Piping

Piping is a great way to give a neat finish to pillow (cushion) seams and it's easier than it looks! You will need to use a zipper or piping foot on your machine.

1 Cut 2 in. (5 cm) wide strips across the bias of the fabric (diagonally). Cutting on the bias means that the fabric will stretch slightly around curves and you won't get wrinkles forming.

2 Fit the zipper or piping foot on to your machine.

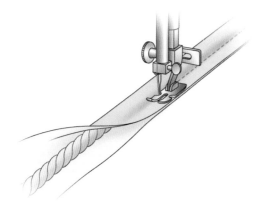

3 To cover the cord, place the piping cord down the center of the bias strip on the wrong side. Bring the long edges of the bias strip together around the cord and stitch down the length close to the cord, using the side of the foot as a guide.

4 If the ends of the cord need to be joined, unpick the machine stitching on the piping for about 2 in. (5 cm) at each end, and fold back the bias strip. Trim each end of the piping so that the ends of the cord will butt up against one another, then bind the ends together with thread. Turn under ¼ in. (6 mm) at one end of the bias strip and slip this over the raw end. Baste (tack) in place close to the cord.

Trimming seam allowances

When sewing sharp-angled corners or circles, you will need to trim the seams before pressing them open, to get a neat finish.

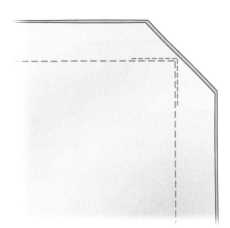

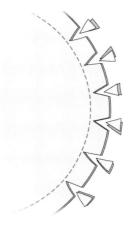

To create a sharp, neat angle, cut across the corner of the seam allowances as shown, close to the stitching, but making sure that you do not cut through the actual stitching. When turning your seam to the right side, use a pair of small, pointed scissors or a knitting needle to carefully push out the point, making sure that you do not push too hard and form a hole.

Notching or clipping curved seams

Notches are small wedges of fabric cut from the seam allowances of outward curves, as shown here, to allow them to lie smooth and flat. On inward curves you only need to clip into the seam allowances so that the edges will spread out and lie flat. Use a small pair of sharp, pointed scissors, to notch or clip at regular intervals, taking care to cut close to but not through the stitches.

Stitches

There are a few stitches used in the projects, to provide a neat seam or a decorative finish.

Backstitch

Bring the needle up through the fabric and take a short backward stitch on the stitching line. Bring the needle through again a stitch-length in front of the first stitch. Take the needle back down where it first came through, and repeat along the stitching line.

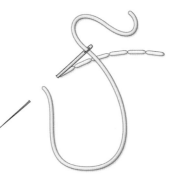

Slipstitch

Slipstitch is nearly invisible and is used to sew up a gap in a seam from the right side of the fabric

Working from right to left, bring the needle through one folded edge of fabric, slip the needle through the fold of the opposite edge for about ¼ in. (6 mm), and draw the needle and thread through. Continue in this way to join both edges.

Blanket stitch

Blanket stitch is a simple but decorative way to finish an edge of fabric.

1 Bring the needle through at the edge of the fabric.

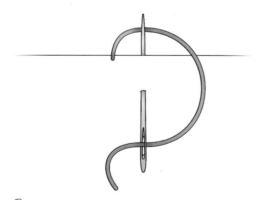

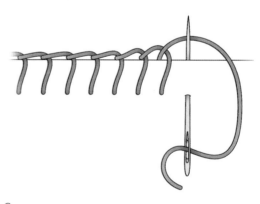

2 Push the needle back through the fabric, a short distance from the edge, and loop the thread under the needle.

3 Make another stitch to the right of this and again loop the thread under the needle. Continue along the fabric and finish with a few small stitches or a knot on the underside.

index

acknowledgments

Thanks to my family and friends who have helped enormously during the production of this book, particularly Jonathan Oxborrow for his patience, for driving a car full of finished projects to London on his day off, and for not minding my blue hands when my rubber gloves developed a hole.

Thank you especially to my parents for their support, for teaching me to have no fear, to "always try something or you'll always wonder what might have happened," and for stepping in when I need extra help.

Thanks also to my "craft consultants" Lynne Pratt and Jenny Tidman for helping me decide on projects, Samantha Hayes for getting me into natural dyes all those years ago—I'll never forgive you!—and Christina Hamilton for generously letting me use her Heart Garland pattern. Thanks to Nigel and Julie "Sweetpea" Smith for finding me buckets, bowls, jugs, and pans along with many other requests, making me believe that they can find absolutely anything, and to Paddy Peters and Helen Brown for inspiring me with their beautiful pottery and love of nature.

A special thank you must go to all at Alder Carr Farm, who have been so friendly and helpful while we were moving the shop to its present location in an old windmill on the farm. Nick and Joan Hardingham kindly allowed us to use the farm for some of the photography—we couldn't ask for a prettier backdrop.

Thank you to everyone at CICO Books, who have all worked so hard to make this beautiful book! Particularly Penny Craig, Sally Powell, and Gillian Haslam who have all been so patient and supportive. Thank you to Gavin Kingcome for his stunning photography, professionalism, and dedication. One day we'll stop laughing about him falling in the pond... and finally, thank you to Cindy Richards, who saw the beauty of indigo and how it could be used to decorate our homes.